encounters with
my wisest self

MARK DAVID GERSON

Dialogues with the Divine: Encounters with My Wisest Self

Copyright © 2015, 2019 Mark David Gerson
All rights reserved

No part of this book may be reproduced, stored in a retrieval system or transmitted by any means, electronic, mechanical, photocopying, recording or otherwise, without written permission from the author, except for the inclusion of brief quotations in critical reviews and certain other noncommercial uses permitted by copyright law.

First Paperback Edition 2015. Second Edition 2019.

Published by MDG Media International
2370 W. State Route 89a
Suite 11-210
Sedona, AZ 86336

www.mdgmediainternational.com

ISBN: 978-1-950189-11-3

Cover Photograph: Kathleen Messmer
www.kathleenmessmer.com

Author Photograph: Kevin Truong
www.kevintruong.com

More information on the author
www.markdavidgerson.com

Resources for Writers
Books, Recordings, Coaching/Mentoring, Workshops/Retreats

*Whenever I feel blocked, I open this book,
read a couple of pages and feel inspired again.*
ANNA BLAGOSLAVOVA – MOSCOW, RUSSIA

*Without Mark David's inspiration, example and encouragement, I might
never have had the courage to publish my book.*
NANCY POGUE LATURNER – AUTHOR OF "VOLUNTARY NOMADS"

A highly recommended guide from one of the most creative people around.
WILLIAM C. REICHARD – AUTHOR OF "EVERTIME"

Coaching with Mark David Gerson: Best investment ever!
CHRISTINE FARRIS – DENVER, CO

*I am filled with awe at how easy Mark David has made this.
No more writer's block!*
AZUREL EFRON – SEDONA, AZ

*I owe so much to Mark David! He helped me believe in myself enough
to write the book that got two wrongful murder convictions overturned.*
ESTELLE BLACKBURN – AUTHOR OF "BROKEN LIVES"

Memoirs
*Acts of Surrender: A Writer's Memoir,
Pilgrimage: A Fool's Journey*

*A dynamic read for the creative spirit within each of us.
Positive inspiration at its best.*
HANK BRUCE – AUTHOR OF "PEACE BEYOND ALL FEAR: A TRIBUTE TO
JOHN DENVER'S VISION"

*A book that has the power to awaken, empower and inspire
anyone who reads it.*
MELISSA SHAWN – AUSTIN, TEXAS

*Read it, love it, pass it on and share Mark David's gift
with someone you love.*
PAOLA RIZZATO – HEYSHAM, UK

Self-Help & Personal/Spiritual Growth
*The Way of the Fool, The Way of the Imperfect Fool,
The Book of Messages*

It will transform your life!
REV. BRENDALYN BATCHELOR – UNITY SANTA FE

Simple but powerful!
DAVE KERPEN – AUTHOR OF "THE ART OF PEOPLE"

A book that changes everything that's holding you back!
TED WIGA – SAN FRANCISCO, CA

The Legend of Q'ntana
*The MoonQuest, The StarQuest, The SunQuest,
The Bard of Bryn Doon*

Magic, music and universal truths masterfully woven into a gripping tale.
BETTY DRAVIS – AUTHOR OF "1106 GRAND BOULEVARD"

An exceptional, timeless novel.
"MINDQUEST REVIEW OF BOOKS"

You will love this book!
AMY ROBBINS-WILSON – AUTHOR, SINGER/SONGWRITER

Leaves you turning every single page, hungry for more!
DAVID MICHAEL – AUTHOR OF "THE UNITED SERIES"

The Sara Stories
Sara's Year, After Sara's Year, The Emmeline Papers

Honest and heartfelt. Brilliant!
JOAN CERIO – HOST OF RADIO'S "EARTH ENERGY FORECAST"

Thrilling...bittersweet...triumphant!
DAN STONE – AUTHOR OF "ICE ON FIRE"

A classic in the making!
D'ARCY MAYO – MITTAGONG, AUSTRALIA

*I looked in temples, churches and mosques.
But I found the Divine within my heart.*
RUMI

What we have to become is what we already are.
THOMAS MERTON

To the demons of my past, who are the angels of my present. And to all those whose journeys touched mine in the creation of this book. Bless you all.

Contents

Foreword	9
Genesis	15
Revelation	45
Acts	91
Exodus	157
Blessed Transformation	225
Afterword	229
Dialogues with Your Divine	231
Grateful Appreciation	241

Foreword

The "dialogues" in this book emerged from the silence and solitude of a fiery autumn and frozen winter. I had just moved a hundred miles north from Toronto to the rural outskirts of Penetanguishene, a summer-resort town on the shores of Lake Huron. For the fifth time in two years, I had packed my few belongings and followed my heart along the asphalt road of my soul's journey.

Why was I there? If I needed a reason for the world, it was to work on my novel, *The MoonQuest*. Whatever else materialized, I hoped that a fourth draft would. After all, *The MoonQuest*'s earlier drafts had been largely written during just such a time of retreat.

Although *The MoonQuest* was a constant theme during those five months, I made little progress on it. Instead, even as I struggled to move the novel forward, other words came, and I soon found myself being propelled on an unexpected journey of healing through writing.

Mine was a heart-sickness — neither physical nor life-threatening. But it was soul- and spirit-threatening. For without trusting that it was safe to let the world more fully into my heart and my heart more fully into my words, I could never take my writing and life to deeper levels, never fully live the precepts I taught in my seminars and workshops.

I have always seen creative writing as a metaphor for creative living, believing that the principles that work for one unfailingly work for the other: faith, trust, surrender and openheartedness; vulnerability, truthfulness and flow. And, of course, being in the moment.

Opposing all of these is fear.

If fear no longer paralyzes me, it still occasionally slows me down. It's the core issue of our time, triggering everything from writer's block to war. It's the only barrier to flow — of words, of abundance, of life, of love.

Many layers of fear had dissolved for me by the time I installed myself at 296 Champlain Road two days before my forty-second birthday. But more healing awaited, as it always does.

Opportunities for growth arise out of every breath when we are open to them. Often they arise most clearly when we step into the stillness. For me, this place of stillness was a sparsely furnished one-bedroom flat across the road from the spirit-filled waters of Georgian Bay. Sharing my rear wall was a larger house, home to Angela and Jim Emery and their nine-year-old son, Jeremy. Jeremy instantly adopted me and my cocker spaniel, Roxy, and his outpouring of unconditional love was among the first challenges — and opportunities — of this journey. Others followed in rapid succession, relating as much to my life as to my writing.

Meditative or inner dialogue is a technique I have often taught in my writing workshops. Once in a meditative state, you ask a question and then allow the answers to emerge through what I call "writing on the Muse Stream" — setting pen to paper or fingers to keyboard and letting the words flow through you onto the page, without stopping for judgment, censorship, editing, correction or second thoughts. Whether you believe the answers come from God, your Muse or a deeper part of yourself, they do come...when you let them.

My first written words of that five-month retreat came as inner dialogue, though not one that my conscious mind had initiated. Instead, as I sat in meditation one morning, I heard the words, "I just want to say something." It was an echo of a recent nightmare and when I engaged it in conversation, I discovered a part of me that I had unwittingly denied.

By mid-January, these occasional dialogues were surging out of me, sometimes two or three times a day, and "dialogue with the divine" had replaced "inner dialogue" as the heading in my journal.

Generally, the first words of dialogue came the moment I closed my eyes. When that happened, I reached for my pad and, eyes still shut, recorded what I heard, sensed, experienced. More often than not, the power of the words evaded me. At times I resented them. In that respect, I was no different from my writing-workshop participants who, when writing for the first time from a place of heart and truth, often reject their work as meaningless or pedestrian. It wasn't until later, as I typed and read over the day's writing, that I began to sense its transformative power.

Through this ongoing dialogue and the experiences that sparked it, I began to open my heart wider and wider still, to trust deeply and more deeply still, to surrender more and more completely to a wisdom and divinity I had never before acknowledged. Through them I began to embrace more fully my vision, my power, my strength and my truth. Through them I began to discover new ways to write, new ways to teach, new ways to live, new ways to be.

I had set out to write a different book. I tried to write that other book. Instead, this one appeared — not initially as a book, but simply as an outlet for all that floated into consciousness.

Who is the Divine? What was the presence I engaged when this book spilled out of me? It is the presence that resides in all of us... the light that shines in and through each of us...the presence that infuses everything and everyone at all times and in all ways. There are many names for it: Muse, God/Goddess, Infinite Mind, Great Spirit, Higher Self or, as I put it in the book's subtitle, Wisest Self. In short, it is the Divine, part of each of us and all of us, yet at the same time something of which we are all part.

Who was I speaking to? Who was speaking to me? That still small voice that is not really small at all. It is the largest, deepest, truest part of ourselves, if we but open to it, honor it, embrace it, choose to accept its oneness with us. That is the Divine who came to me — to whom I opened the totality of my being in order to access and receive these inspiring words. That is the divinity we all share, the divinity we can all touch as we write and live.

My dialogues with the Divine began out of need — not the need to write a book, but the need to reconnect with my wholeness and my heart. I share them with you now, knowing that my words are your words, my fears are your fears, my strength and courage are yours, as is my love and wisdom. For we are all one beneath the skin of individuality. We are all one in the divinity and divine presence of love.

Who is the Divine? It is you, me, God, the flowers in your garden, the trees in your yard, the kitten that cuddles on your lap as you read these words. It is the very words themselves. May they move, guide and inspire you as they did and still do me. And may you move from them to your own direct links with your own divinity.

"Dialogues" – Why Now?

I made many attempts, through the five years that followed the completion of these dialogues, to get them published. But no agent or publisher felt moved to take them on. For a time, my then wife and I crafted a line of popular magnets that married my artwork with inspirational sayings from *Dialogues,* and in *Acts of Surrender: A Writer's Memoir* I tell of how one of those magnets attracted the publishing interest of Neale Donald Walsch. Alas, that too went nowhere.

After a time, other enthusiasms and other books captured my attention, and *Dialogues with the Divine* moved into the musty recesses of my computer's hard drive. It was a project whose time I believed to have passed, subsumed, in a sense, by my *Acts of Surrender* memoir.

Ironically, it was *Acts of Surrender* that revived it. At a time when I was already revisiting my past — revising and expanding *The Voice of the Muse: Answering the Call to Write* — a UK fan of *Acts of Surrender* sent me a note on Facebook: "You mention *Dialogues with the Divine* in your memoir," she wrote, "but I can't find it anywhere. Where can I get a copy?"

"Unpublished," I wrote back, "and likely to remain so."

Even as I hit send, I began to suspect that this reader had been channeling my Muse and that it might finally be time to dust off *Dialogues with the Divine*. To be honest, I wasn't initially keen on resuscitating a book that, in some ways, was even more personally raw than *Acts of Surrender* had been. Then I reread my original Foreword, and I was hooked.

For this edition of *Dialogues with the Divine*, I have streamlined the text to eliminate redundancy and revised or updated some of the references for clarity. I have also added a new section to help you access your own divine wisdom and experience dialogues of your own. Other than that, this final draft is not much different from its most recent predecessor, a version I had not looked at in more than a decade.

When I did look it again, I found it both inspiring and disturbing — inspiring because most of the wise words of my divinity are still relevant; disturbing because many of the fearful words of my eighteen-years-ago self are also still relevant!

But as these dialogues reminded me then and remind me again now, we live our lives as a spiral: When it feels as though we are being pummeled by issues we thought we had long ago resolved, we must remember that life's spiral returns us not to our starting point, but to a place above it — to a new beginning at a heightened level of consciousness.

As such, this *Dialogues with the Divine* spiral has, mercifully, not returned me to 1996. Rather, it has propelled me forward, freeing me to move through and past deeper expressions of the core fears I experienced through that winter of introspection and retreat. To paraphrase the Toshar of my *MoonQuest*, I have allowed the Mark I was to touch — and teach — the Mark David I have become. If reexperiencing these dialogues has often been discomfiting, it has always been profoundly healing. May it be so for you too.

Genesis

I arrived in Penetanguishene early on the afternoon of my forty-second birthday, still unsure why I had felt called to be here. Fall was already drawing to a close this far north, and as it stripped the trees of their gold and crimson leaves, it stripped me too — leaving me as bare and vulnerable as the oaks, birches and maples that clambered up the treed slopes behind my new home. This was to be a new beginning for me...a genesis...

Wednesday, October 9, 1996
PREDAWN

I am barely asleep two hours when I awake in a drenching, dry-mouth sweat. Woven mantra-like through vague nightmare-memories of meaningless death, violence and betrayal is the phrase, "I just want to say something." The line, emblematic of longstanding blocks to my self-expression, keeps me awake until just before dawn, when I reach for pen and paper and start to write.

While my primary attraction at this time remains to men, as it has through my adult life, I have proclaimed myself open to a relationship with a woman, at least in theory. In practice, it feels as though the idea threatens not only my sexual identity but one of the few anchoring certainties I feel I have left.

What do you mean, "I just want to say something"? What is it you want to say?

I want to speak truth.

Truth is frightening.

I just want to say something.

I'm afraid.

I have to speak. Why do you keep me silent?

I'm afraid.

That's not good enough. I need to speak, to communicate, to speak my truth. Our truth. I have been stilled too long. I am going to explode. You must let me speak. I have to speak.

I'm afraid, afraid of what you'll say, of what it will mean, of what it will do, of how it will change me, of how it will change everything.

> Everything has already changed. Everything will continue to change. Always. It cannot be otherwise.

I know that, intellectually. I can accept that, intellectually. But these coming changes don't feel incremental. They feel monumental. Irreversible. So I'm afraid…of what I don't know, of what I can't see, of what I can't imagine…of what I can imagine.

> What do you imagine?

Married with kids.

> That may or may not happen. Would it be so bad?

No. Yes and no. All at the same time.

> And?

There's more. I know it. I feel it. You're pulling me closer to my essence and it terrifies me. If someone goes after one of my masks, I'm not destroyed. There's only a chink in that one mask, and there are still others. But strip away all my masks and all that's left is my essence. I will have to show it, reveal it, expose it. Expose me. I won't be able to retreat. I will have no mask to hide behind. I'll be destroyed.

> So you would hide that essence, that beautiful, golden white light — even from yourself?

It feels safer that way. If I can't get at it, no one can.

> This can't go on. That is not why you are here. You are here to speak. You are here to write. You are here to communicate. You are here to communicate truth.

I know. But I'm frightened. How do I make it safe?

There is no safety outside yourself. Your only safety is within. Your only safety is your truth. It will set you free, if you let it, if you surrender to it. Be afraid, if fear you must. But don't let fear stop you — from speaking, from writing, from communicating, from being. If you do, you might as well stop breathing.

You have done so much, come so far. Don't squander all you have achieved by stopping now. Don't give up on yourself. Don't give up on the world. Don't give up on the light. That light is your courage. Reach down, deep down, to tap into it. See how it sparkles when you touch it. So, too, will you sparkle when you come out of hiding and share the light of your courage and the courage of your truth with the world.

The world needs it. The world needs you. The time is right. The place is right. So shine your light into the fear, and let that light carry you through your fear, to the other side of fear. Have you been let down yet?

No.

Have you been abandoned yet?

No.

Then release the past upon which so many of these fears are based. Release it and let it go. And feel the lightness, feel the freedom. Feel your safety in the certainty that you are protected and guided by eternal love. That support is here for you always, every minute of every hour of every day. Trust that you will be taken care of, in all ways, and you will be.

What do I do?

Be. Listen. Trust. Act when the time is right. Write and speak of your experiences when the time is right. Communicate your truth. Above all don't let fear rule you. Don't be its slave.

What do I write? What do I speak? What do I say?

The answers will come, in time. When they do, don't run from them. Be open to them. Trust them. Now, be still. Be with these words. Just be.

Thank you. I'm still afraid…but thank you.

Namaste.[1]

---

[1] A Hindi word derived from the Sanskrit, meaning "I honor the Divine in you."

Saturday, November 2, 1996
EVENING

My friend Barbara Sauvé is in the area revisiting her childhood roots. Her weeks-long presence has been a joy and a challenge — the joy of sharing my journey with a fellow spiritual traveler; the challenge of not measuring my process and progress against hers, of not judging myself as inadequate. Now, Barbara prepares to continue her quest elsewhere.

Knowing I must stay behind, I feel stuck, my emotions intensified by guilt and shame over my desire to eat my way through my anxiety. I have never been overweight, never suffered from a conventional eating disorder. But it is always too easy for me to stuff my emotions with food. It is always too easy for stress to upset my digestion.

I'm afraid. Confused. Angry. Frustrated. Lonely. Defeated. I don't want to feel this way. I want to feel happy. Joyous. Fulfilled. I want to express myself creatively, sexually, visually. Instead I feel stuck in Penetanguishene and stuck in my emotions. Barbara succeeded and she's leaving. If I'm staying, I must have failed somehow. I know it's futile to compare my journey with hers. But I can't stop myself. And I can't stop myself from wanting to eat, even as I know it will never fill the void.

Why is everyone so much stronger than I am? There I go, comparing again. Judging again. It's not relevant. Yet I have spent so much of my life in relative terms that it's hard to break the habit. So here I am. I need help.

> You have all the strength you need, all the courage you need, all the fearlessness you need.

Intellectually, you'll get no argument. But I don't feel it. I feel frightened. I feel all the things I opened this dialogue with and I don't know what to do.

> It is what you told Barbara this afternoon: It is not about doing. It is about being. You are doing fine. You climb mountains, cross boundaries, face demons, conquer heights others can only dream of.

Then why is it so difficult?

> If it were easy, everyone would do it. You have the strength for this journey. You have the courage for this journey. You have the faith for this journey. Trust in the journey. Trust yourself. Trust these words you write. For in trusting them, you trust yourself.

I do...but enough?

> There is no "not enough." There is always enough. Everything you need resides within you, waiting to be tapped...longing to be tapped. Tap into it. Touch it. Embrace your remarkable strength, your indefatigable courage. Touch all you are and you will touch the source of these words.

Who are you? What is the source of these words?

> I am All, the totality of everything. I am God. I am the Divine. I am all that is and ever will be. I am love. I am hope. I am compassion. I am understanding. I am mercy. I am forgiveness. I am patience. And I am you, your wisest self. There is no separation between you and me, for there is only and ever one. There is no separation between what you write here and who you are, for there is only and ever one. There can never be any separation, for there is no separation. Separateness is a human construct, an illusion.

I don't feel any better.

> You will. Give it time. Sit. Sit patiently, in peace. Empty your mind. Open your heart. Open your heart to these words you

write and you will open your heart to yourself — to the beauty and light within you. Reach out and touch your wisdom and divinity. Reach within and embrace it. Be the God that you are, the divinity that you are, the wisdom that you are. Be it. Be.

Thank you. I will try.

Don't try. Just be.

You make it sound so simple.

It is, even if "simple" is not always "easy." Trust in that simplicity. Believe in it. Believe in yourself — in the simplicity of your wisdom, in the glory of your divinity and in the beauty of your truth. Be that wisdom. Be that divinity. Be that truth. Why do you resist it? Why do you resist yourself?

Fear.

Feel the fear and let it go. Let it be. Let yourself be. Listen to the song playing in your head, the song you heard at Unity.

I can't remember all the words.

Remember the words you can. Remember the spirit. Their truth will illuminate and complete whichever fragments you remember.

"I am love. I am joy. I am the light divine."

That is all you need to know. That is all you need to be. For that is all of what you are. Can you open your heart and mind to that?

I don't know…

I sit quietly, but my mind refuses to empty. Instead, thoughts of suicide flutter through. I wonder who will find me. I wonder what will happen to Roxy until I'm found…after I'm found. As these thoughts come, thoughts of ending my life go, and I release them both gladly and reluctantly.

Moments later, I feel a sense of my late mother's presence and hear in my mind the song she often sang to me when I was little: "I love you, a bushel and a peck / A bushel and a peck and a hug around the neck / A hug around the neck and a barrel and a heap / A barrel and a heap and I'm talking in my sleep / About you." I hear the song and feel better. Not all better. Not even a lot better. But better, which is better than before.

Tuesday, November 26, 1996
AFTERNOON

The first two times my friend and mentor Carole H. Leckner asks me to teach her Toronto creative writing course, I decline. Then I have a dream. In it, a woman named Beth is seriously injured when her jeep strikes a land mine. Later in her hospital room, her husband begs her not to teach. "It's too dangerous," George argues. Beth will not be moved. "I must teach," she cries. As I wake up, I know that I too have no choice but to teach.

Teaching Carole's course leads to workshops of my own, which lead in turn to The MoonQuest, *a novel I write as I teach: in total trust and surrender, knowing nothing of the story except as it emerges onto the page from one day to the next. The story? Four travelers led by Toshar set off on a quest for M'nor, a moon not seen in their land since storytelling was outlawed and storytellers condemned to death. Their mission: to trigger M'nor's long-prophesied Return.*

Encouraging my own Return — if only to The MoonQuest, *whose barely started fourth draft I have not looked at in months — are the open-mic readings I participate in at The Daily Perk, a cafe in the neighboring town of Midland. I am to read again tomorrow, and I am already anxious about it.*

Panic, sort of. I know I'm moving toward my own Return...to *The MoonQuest*. I'm resisting. I'm frightened. I don't know what to do.

> You do know. You have written how, in *The MoonQuest*. You have spoken how, in your writing workshops. Your words have told you how and tell you again. Your words are your teachers. Each word teaches you so much. Don't run from your words any more than you would run from your teachers. Let them teach you. Let

them show you. Word by word. Thought by thought. Moment by moment. Silence by silence.

It's the silence. Is that what I fear? It's one of the things I fear.

> Never fear the silence. The silence is filled with treasures. It will enrich you, enrich your work, enrich your life, enrich your love... if you let it.

I don't know what I'm supposed to do. What do I do?

> Do nothing. Be.

I just can't sit here and have the book write itself—

> No?

Touché. You're right. I need to sit with it. I need to sit and let it come. I know I do. Why does that frighten me so much? Is it the loss of control?

> There is no way to control this process. You must surrender to it, unconditionally.

How do I begin? Where do I begin? What do I write? How do I marry what I have written before with what is yet to come? Do I keep the story in first person or go back to the third person of the first draft? How can I start without even a clue to these questions?

> When you sit in the silence with pen poised, you will know what you need to know. Don't wait for the knowing or the knowing will never come. Begin, and the knowing will follow. Then that knowing will lead you to the next knowing. Trust that.

I want to. I do trust it...but not fully. I'm afraid to surrender. Again. Still.

> You will not fall. You will not fail. You will not hurt yourself, though you will feel pain. The pain will be nothing as to the pain

you will feel if you do nothing, if you write nothing...if you give up and let fear rule you.

I know I can't do that. Yet I feel paralyzed. I feel as though I can't go on, move on, move forward. I feel as though I can't write. Because I don't want to write.

I pause, knowing that my last sentence was a lie.

I do want to write. I need to write. I know that. How can I say I don't want to write? I must write. I must write as much as Beth had to teach. I must teach too. I must start by teaching myself. The only way right now is through my writing. So, again, what do I do?

> Wait until tomorrow night at The Daily Perk. Read what you feel called to read. Listen to what you read. Listen to your own words. Listen and absorb. The words you read are for your audience, of course. But like all words in *The MoonQuest*, your words are first for you. They are teaching words, healing words.
>
> You say you want to heal yourself? Start by writing, by fulfilling your *MoonQuest*, by honoring the M'nor inside you, the light within you. Do it without fear, if you can. Do it with fear if you cannot. For write this story you must. Live it you must. Be it you must. You cannot move, you cannot grow, you cannot fulfill your destiny without this book. This book is you. It is your arms and legs. It is your heart. It is your soul. It is *your* story. Only yours. And tell it you must or, like the Toshar of your *MoonQuest*, you will never be free to move on to other realms, set off on other journeys.
>
> Tomorrow night at The Perk is a threshold, just as your experience there last week was a threshold. Give yourself permission to move through it with courage and ease, and then allow the next phase of your journey — *The MoonQuest* you live as much as *The MoonQuest* you write — to reveal itself, one day at a time.
>
> Trust the journey. Trust your creative process. Trust your strength. Trust these words to guide you.

Thank you. I will try—

    Don't try. Be.

Thank you.

        Namaste.

Thursday, November 28, 1996
2:00AM

I share my MoonQuest *excerpt at The Perk's open-mic night, an excerpt markedly different from any other I have read publicly: It's a sequence of such brutality that part of me cannot believe I wrote it...wishes I hadn't written it. After the reading, a young man approaches me. "Wasn't that a bit too—" he struggles to find the right word, "relentless?" "I'm not in charge of the story," I reply. "The story is in charge of me." He looks at me as though I must be mad.*

A few hours later, I wake from a nightmare. In it, I watch a woman force her way into a classroom, a place she knows she doesn't belong. I sense that she is considering doing something wrong, something that could harm her. "Don't do it!" I cry out. Ignoring me, she walks to a mirror. "If I don't know who I am, how can I play someone else?" she asks her reflection in both sadness and anger. She then wraps toweling around her fist and smashes the mirror. By the end of the dream, I know she is likely dead.

What is this nightmare telling me?

> It is a response to your *MoonQuest* reading at The Perk and to your interchange with the young man.

But what is it telling me?

> You are afraid that you don't fit in and cannot ever belong, that forcing yourself into a place where you don't belong will harm you. You are afraid that self-knowledge will not protect you, that the self-knowledge and inner wisdom that free you to write — to write *The MoonQuest*, for example — will only end up destroying you. You are afraid that truth is dangerous, that expressing and sharing your truth is even more dangerous.

So what do I do? How do I protect myself?

> There is nothing to do, nothing you need to protect. The only thing is to be. To be yourself. To be true to yourself. To be conscious.

Of what?

> Of everything, all the time.

That's impossible.

> Nothing is impossible.

These answers are riddles, just like the nightmare.

> What else do you want to know?

I want to know what dangers I face and how to avoid them.

> Haven't these words just revealed that to you?

Is there more to the dream?

> There is more to every dream. What you have just written is all you need to know for the moment. That, and this: There is no reason for you to feel abandoned. You have not been abandoned. There is no call for you to take measures to protect yourself. You are protected, as protected as you will allow yourself to be. You are safe, as safe as you will allow yourself to be. You are embraced, as embraced as you will allow yourself to be. You are loved, as loved as you will allow yourself to be. Your words and your truth protect you. Whether you write, speak and share them is then a choice — your choice to make. The choices are always yours. That is why it is so important to be conscious and to choose consciously.

I'm afraid.

> Of course you are. But you will be fine. You are on the right track. Just keep your eyes open, your heart open, your mind open. Don't lose sight, inner sight, of your goals, of your stories, of

your destiny. You know your destiny. Don't run from it. Don't turn your back on the healing that has already worked its way through you. You are healing. You *are* healing. Let the healing continue. Don't struggle so. Don't resist so. Let. Let be.

I'm trying.

Don't try so hard. Relax into it. This is not a contest. There are no winners or losers. It is life, and life can be as smooth and free-flowing as you allow it to be. You don't allow enough. You struggle too much. You fight too much. Your struggling and fighting create too much friction. All that friction creates heat, the kind of heat that could lead to an explosion. Replace struggle with surrender. Be aware. Be conscious.

What danger am I facing?

Self-deception. Acknowledge your truth. Accept your truth. Embrace your truth. Live your truth. Express your truth. Your truth is all you have. It is all anyone has. Don't abandon it. Let yourself be taught by it by reading your own words. Read them, then add to them. Add to them to enlighten, to illuminate, to make your truth known...to you as well as to the world.

Write. And in writing you will right so many wrongs, heal so much woundedness...yours and the world's. Don't run from this writing/righting. Embrace it. Be one with it. It is your job, your destiny, your life force. Open your heart to it. Open your loins to it. It is an act of creativity, of self-creation.

Now, return to your bed. Return to sleep. Return to dreams. And choose. Choose life.

I want to. I am. More each day.

Of course you are. Just a reminder.

Good night. And thank you.

Namaste.

Monday, December 23, 1996

AFTERNOON

I sit down to write and begin as I encourage my students to: I set pen to paper and keep the pen moving regardless of what comes out. To help prime and maintain the flow, I use free association, a favorite tool because it's playful and it forces the logical, judgmental, hypercritical, fear-based part of my mind to stand aside. It also forces me to abandon control and surrender to the seeming chaos of the present moment.

One word. Two words. Now three words. Where is the story? That's four. Where is the story? Where is *The MoonQuest*? Where does it hide? Why does it hide? Why does it hide from me? Why do I hide from it? What am I afraid of? Why do I run? And hide? Hide. Hidden. Concealed. Congealed. The story has congealed within me. How do I thaw it out, get it out, let it out? Out, damn spot! Spot. Stain. Tache. Tâche[2]. Task. Tusk. Husk. Grain. Grain of sand. Leader of the band. How grand.

> Come. Come ride tonight.

What? Where?

> Wherever your heart carries you. Wherever it will let you carry it. Wherever you will let it carry you. Up into the stars. Down beneath the earth. Deep in forests dense and tangled. Out over oceans wild. Let it go. Let go all expectations, all destinations. Let go all that holds you back. Step into the black, into the black beyond which nothing is. Where nothing is, everything lies. Treasures beyond imagining— You force. Don't force. Let. Let be. Don't bumble. Accept the stumble. Accept the jumble. Accept the jungle.

---

2 "Tache" is the French word for "stain"; "tâche" is French for "task."

I'm afraid.

> So you are afraid. Your fear cannot get in the way unless you let it. You are in charge. This is your destiny, your journey. A journey of love. Self-love.

A journey of fear.

> Through fear. Past fear. Beyond fear. Into light, spirit, essence. Self. Oneness.

What is my essence? Why can't I touch it?

> You touch it every day. Every hour. Every moment. Every breath. When you breathe. When you remember to breathe. You touch it always. You don't always choose to feel it, to see it. Choose. It is all about choice. Make the choices that are true, that speak truth. Then you will know your essence. Then you will experience your essence. Then you will be your essence. Then you will be.

Be. Be. Be. Be. Be. Bee. Bea. Aunt Bea. Bumble bee. Sting. Stung. Sing. Sung. Mung bean. Been. Has been. To be. To be or not to be; that is the question. That is the only question. The sole question. The soul question. Quest-ion. Ask and you shall find. You shall receive. You shall be. Be. Be. Be. Be. Be still. Don't kill. What a thrill. Cowboy Bill. Up the hill. To fetch a pail of water. Water. Waiter. Wait. Don't wait. *Don't wait!* Weight. Weighty. Heavy. He ain't heavy, he's my brother. Bother. Don't bother. No bother. No other. No otter. Sea otter. Play! No play, no pay. Not today. *Oy vey.* This is nonsense. No sense. No cents. I'm tired.

> Then sleep.

I should write.

> Un-*should*-er.

My neck is sore.

> Don't go break-neck.

What the heck. Dreck. I'm writing dreck. Shit. Garbage. Trash. Tish. Tush. Tosh. Holy gosh. What bosh. What does this mean? Why am I just spinning pages of crap, when I should be writing with a capital W? Serious writing. Not uncomfortable writhing. Why can't I heal?

> Healing is a process. You are a work-in-process. You are healing. Look at you. Look back. Look back three months. See how your heart is healing, how your voice is healing, how every part of you is healing.

It never seems to end.

> No, it doesn't.

I'm tired.

> Then rest. Do your best. Don't flee the nest. Stay on the quest. That's the best.

The best the best the best. This is taking me nowhere.

> It has taken you where you needed to go, where you need to be. There is nothing more to do. You have written. Pat on the back.

For this…this…dreck?

> No expression of self, however confused or tentative is dreck. It is power — expressed power, powerful expression. Honor it. And honor you where you are in this moment. Let go expectation. Just be. Rest time now. Nap time. Sleep time. Dream time.

Saturday, January 4, 1997
AFTERNOON

Again, I find myself using food to numb my anxiety: I prepare a pot of herbal tea and a slice of Angela Emery's homemade Christmas stollen. One slice becomes two, then three — not savored but wolfed down with compulsive fistfuls of trail mix. Tea, a small sweet and a book: a ritual I have long treasured, one with unwritten rules about how much I can eat and drink. Now, I realize, there can be no rules, only moment-to-moment awareness. Suddenly, the phrase "I'm out of control" replaces every sentence on the page of the book I'm reading until I allow my eyes to close and this dialogue to emerge.

I'm out of control. I'm afraid...afraid of the emptiness. I'm afraid it will devour me, destroy me, annihilate me. I'm afraid if I don't stay full, I will die.

You won't, you know.

I don't believe that.

The emptiness is a gift.

I don't believe that either.

When did this start? Do you remember?

No. Yes. I don't know. Food is love. Food is Mummy's love.

I sense my mother's presence and hear her voice, which then merges into the voice of my wisest self.

No, it isn't. Food is not my love. My love — whatever it was in the past — is ever-present, constant. My love exists as strongly in the emptiness as it does in the fullness. Don't hate yourself. Whatever was done to you, whatever was withheld from you — that was the past. Food can never replace that. All the food in the world cannot replace that. Physical fullness cannot replace that.

Then nothing can. I'm doomed. I might as well be dead.

It is food that deadens you. Not all food. Not food consciously eaten. Not food enjoyed. You did not enjoy that cake you consumed just now, did you?

No.

And now you are consumed by guilt.

Yes.

Let go the guilt, for a start. Don't waste your energy on guilt or regret. Learn, instead. Learn from the experience. Grow from it. Heal from it. Then move on.

I don't know how.

You do. The answer is not abstinence or rules or the illusion of control. The answer is consciousness, responsibility and love. Self-love.

How can I love this...this...this misfit that no one loved?

My mother's voice again; it again merges into the voice of my wisest self.

I loved you. I love you still. My love cannot replace the nourishment your body needs. It cannot and need not. But my love is here for you, always. The past is passed. Let go whatever was. Let it go and love your present as you prepare for your future. Face the void. Be with the emptiness. Be the emptiness.

I don't know what to do, how to deal with it, how to heal myself.

The healing comes. It emerges out of love, out of self-love. Be conscious. Be aware. Don't punish yourself. Don't strain. Be. Be in your power. Be your power. Be your wisdom. Be your divinity. Be your love.

I feel helpless. I don't want this to control me. But I'm afraid of the emptiness. Emptiness is death.

Out of death comes new life, wondrous new life. With it comes new light, new love, new creation. With it comes renewed power, renewed wisdom, renewed empowerment. Don't dilute your power. Don't run from it. Don't eat a wall of fear around it. Love the emptiness. Embrace the dark. Enter into the dark. It will not kill you. It will give you life.

But what do I do?

Do nothing. Sit in the stillness and listen to your heart. Your heart's voice is your divinity. Your heart's voice is your power. Your heart's voice is your light and your healing. Don't punish yourself. Don't act from fear or guilt. Act from love, from self-love.

It sounds hard.

It is simple but not always easy. You can heal this fear. But only if you will it so.

I do. I choose to be healed. I choose to heal myself. I choose to assume my place in the world, my place of healing, my place of power. I will it.

Then the God that you are wills it for you and with you. With your conscious help, this shall heal.

Thank you. I wish this was the end of it. It's only the beginning.

The beginning of the end. The end is in sight. Trust that.

I do. Thank you.

Remember, you are love. Life is love. And love is healing.

Thank you.

In the moments that follow, I fall into an old pattern and begin to formulate new rules around food and eating. Then I hear this:

No rules. Just be with the moment. Be in the moment. And trust.

I will it. I don't want to control. I don't want to be controlled. I choose to take charge of my own life, my own beingness. I choose to surrender to my wisdom, my divinity and my truth. I choose love.

If you choose it, it will be. If you will it, it is.

Monday, January 6, 1997
MORNING

I hate myself this morning — for not writing, for not having the courage to face the blank page, for not having the wisdom to know what to do with The MoonQuest.

From a long-ago meditation: I see myself clinging to the roof-ledge of a skyscraper as I hear a voice urging me to let go. I try but I can't. Instead, I hold on even more fearfully. Over the next days, I meditatively revisit this experience until I finally muster the courage to release my grip. To my amazement, I float down into what I can only describe as the arms of God.

Why can't I trust? Why am I so immobilized by fear of the emptiness? By *my* emptiness? Why do I resist putting pen to paper? Not only for *The MoonQuest* but for something like this? I'm lazy. No, I'm terrified...by my own power. What will happen if I let it out? The world as I know it will collapse, explode, implode, cease to exist. Whatever modicum of safety I have managed to carve for myself will be shattered. I know I have been through this before and have come out okay. Better than okay: I am stronger and wiser now than I have ever been. Yet here I am, still curled up in womb-like paralysis. Hiding. Not wanting to move, to see, to be seen.

I never thought I would say this, but I speak more easily than I write. That's probably because I can control who I speak what to. I can't control who will ultimately read my words. Is it that loss of control that paralyzes me so much this morning as I think about writing?

I think it's also the idea of launching into the void afresh every day. With previous drafts of *The MoonQuest*, I followed where the story took me from one day to the next, and the story always emerged in sequence, in order. This new draft is demanding a new level of surrender from me because everything I write is out of sequence...out of order...out of control. That means I can no longer use yesterday's writing as a launching pad to today's. Now, it's a new launch every day, a new leap into the void every day. It's more than I can handle. It's more than I can cope with. It's—

> Like waking up to each new day?

Ouch. Maybe. I want control. I want a safety net. I want to know I won't fall. I want to know I won't be shot down.

> You cannot know that. All you can do is trust. All you can do is trust that you will always be caught, supported and embraced in the arms of God.

Even that doesn't feel enough right now.

> Then don't write. Put *The MoonQuest* aside.

Then I feel guilty, unworthy, slothful, like a sissy-ninny-scaredy-cat. Then I'm filled with self-loathing, thinking I should be doing something I'm not, that I should be able to do something I can't.

> What about letting go the shoulds, just like you tell your students to do? What about acknowledging that perhaps you are not quite ready to return to *The MoonQuest*?

It's so hard to have clarity on this. It's so hard to know when I'm running away and when I'm respecting my needs and capacities of the moment. There is so much baggage in the way. So many layers of not wanting to see, of being afraid to see, of just plain fear, blocking my vision.

> Don't be so hard on yourself. Perhaps you are moving toward a return to *The MoonQuest* but are not there yet? Perhaps this is part of the process?

Maybe it is time to return, and I'm letting fear stop me.

And maybe you are beating yourself up. Let it go. Take the pressure off yourself. This is not about production. This is not about performance. This is not about perfection. This is about passion not discipline. This is about growth. This is about truth. This is about healing. The healing will happen. The healing is happening. One day's delay, one week's delay — one year's delay — will not stop the process…cannot stop the process. You continue to be so hard on yourself — still. You expect perfection — still. Let go all that. Let go and the words and scenes will come. Let go and the fear will go. Remember the joy you have experienced while writing. It can be yours again.

How?

By easing off. By stripping away expectation. By stripping away pressure. By loving yourself — where you are right now, not where you think you should be. This is your journey. No one else's. Don't compare. Don't judge. You judge yourself and you find yourself wanting. You are not. You are powerful beyond measure. What you will can be yours.

I'm afraid to will it.

Today, perhaps. Right now, maybe. But you have willed it before and you shall again. Like Toshar, you are afraid to assume your mantle of power, your birthright as healer and storyteller. Yet assume it you must. As long as you choose truth, there is no other option. Respect your journey. Love yourself. Trust your divinity. And all will follow from that.

What do I do now?

Nothing. Sit. Be still. Be patient. And trust.

EVENING

It's April 1994. Just as I will feel called to move to Penetanguishene in two years, I now feel powerfully drawn to Nova Scotia — a call I imagine will take me five years to answer. Then something odd happens: As I more fully embrace my Nova Scotia dream, my anticipated time frame collapses in on itself again and again. In the end, I arrive on the Atlantic coast, having wound down my business and sold virtually all I own, in five months not five years.

The void between dinner and bedtime can be the most difficult one for me to enter into. On this evening all I want to do is eat, to keep filling the temporal and emotional voids with food. When the feelings become too difficult to bear, I turn to meditation and the blank page for support and guidance.

I can't keep living this way.

> Nor could you continue to live the old way. This is a transition you experience, a necessary transition. It will pass. It will pass and you will emerge even stronger and more powerful — more alive with your own power, your own mission, your own calling to heal.

All well and good. It's *now* that causes me grief.

> Face your fear with courage. You have immense pools of courage… great, unplumbed depths of courage, of *coeur*, of heart. Listen to your heart. At first it may be difficult to hear what it says. But in time, as you listen, as you choose to listen, as you open yourself to its wisdom, the voice of your heart will ring true and clear like a cathedral bell. This, like everything else, is a process, one to which you must surrender yourself, one to which you have already begun to surrender yourself. Give yourself a great pat on the back for that. More than that: Give yourself a great hug.

It feels like I'm failing, like I'm flailing.

> It always feels like flailing at the beginning. First steps, though seemingly minuscule, are always the most difficult. But even the tiniest steps, however halting, deserve recognition. So acknowledge your accomplishments, though you may be tempted to dismiss them as too minor to note. They are not minor at all. You have launched a process that many cannot. You have dared. Be in awe at the strength of character, at the courage that has allowed you to take even these infant steps. From baby steps come larger ones, then larger. Then, before you realize it, you are striding away from this issue with confidence and strength.

It's so hard. I feel lost.

> Of course you do. You kick away yet another pillar of your sense of beingness. It has never been a real pillar. It is rotten on the inside and offers no real support. It is nothing but a hollowed crutch that would collapse were you to put any real weight on it. Kick away that illusion. Leave it behind. Move forward on your own strength, your own power.
>
> Soon, food will no longer be a crutch, a suffocating blanket for your emotions. Soon, you will feel your emotions more fully, experience them more vibrantly. You cannot now imagine what you will see, feel and experience. The glow! The vibrancy! The energy!

What about now? The future sounds wonderful, but I can't get there if I can't get through the now.

> Of course. But it is also important for you to be aware of the wonders and glories that await you. As for the now, be in it. Don't expect miracles overnight. Yet know that each step moves you faster than you can imagine. Remember Nova Scotia? Remember how each acknowledgment of its possibility brought it closer? The same is true here. The same is true of every step you take. Each acknowledgment that your desired outcome is possible,

each acknowledgment that you desire and will it, brings it closer, speeds you along until the healing comes, until the worst is past and all is well. Trust that. Remember and trust.

Thank you. I choose to reclaim my power. I choose fearlessness. I will it.

Revelation

Even as winter deepened in these first weeks of nineteen ninety-seven, the days were subtly lengthening. Spring was edging nearer, and the promise of a new season brought with it not only new insights but the first hints of a new book...a book that, like The MoonQuest, *I didn't at first know I was writing.*

Thursday, January 9, 1997
MORNING

This day for the first time, "Dialogue with the Divine" writes itself above the day's journaling, and it is as though the title itself un-dams a flood of inspirational treasures. Over the next weeks, dialogue begets dialogue and without my conscious awareness, the book I don't yet know is a book begins to write itself. For the moment, though, the only book on my mind remains The MoonQuest *and I begin this day as so many others, hoping for a new scene as I put pen to paper in those moments of semi-conscious freedom I so often experience before rising to face the world.*

I put pen to paper, and what happens? I tell a story — of light and dark, hope and despair...a story of love...lost, found, lost again and then found for all time. Not a story of romantic love and fairy-tale sweethearts reunited, but a story of self-love, self-respect, self-growth, self-nurturing, self-expression, self-light. That's what I'm all about — a journey to love, to self-love. That's all anything and everyone is about. That's the journey of our times, the journey of our souls: a journey toward union, with the Divine...with the Divine within ourselves— Why am I writing this?

> So you will know. So you will remember. So you will communicate. So you will live. So you will love.

Is this about having a relationship?

> A relationship with the Divine, which is the relationship with yourself and the relationship with All. There is no separateness. There is no two-ness or three-ness or multiple-ness. There is only oneness. See yourself as part of everyone and everything. See everyone and everything as part of you. Only then will you

heal. Only then will the earth heal. Only then will love reign supreme, as it must if humanity is to survive.

I'm confused. Is love the cause of healing or its effect?

> Both. Without love there can be no healing. Without healing there can be no love. Don't look for cause or for effect. Don't look at sequentiality. All is simultaneous. Time as you view it is a false construct. Yesterday, today and tomorrow — they are all one.

If time as we know it has no meaning, does that mean that the healing I seek has already occurred? That the love I seek is already present?

> Now you get it. As soon as you think you are broken, you are healed. As soon as you ask the question, you have the answer. In fact, as soon as the question begins to formulate, the answer is present. All is present, always. Healing is present. Love is present. Wholeness is present. Oneness is present. They are present always all the time.

If that's true, why am I writing this? What am I here for? What am I working toward?

> An acknowledgment that the healing is already present.

And the brokenness?

> It is present only in your lack of acknowledgment of healing's presence. In truth, there is no brokenness. How can there be if wholeness is always present? As for what you are "working toward," there is nothing to work toward, not when you mean "work" in the "arduous labor" sense of the word. That is the meaning you apply to it, no?

Yes.

> You are not here to work. Not in that sense. You are here to be. The only true "work" you have has nothing to do with either

laboriousness or struggle. It is about passion. It is about creation. It is about calling. It is that which you cannot *not* do. It is about expressing your heart's desire in the world. That is both work and play, all at the same time.

Life is not separate compartments — this one for work, that one for play; this one for love, that one for hate; this one for life, that one for death; this one for your human self, that one for your divine self. There is no separateness within your life, just as there is no separateness between you and others. All is woven together into a tapestry of oneness, which is the tapestry of life.

Why do I find that so hard to put into practice?

Because you think too much. Because you try too hard. Because you cast a pall of serious intent over everything, stifling joy and suffocating creation. Because you compartmentalize work and play into distinct units that never connect and thus have no meaning. Only oneness has meaning. Only boundarylessness has meaning.

Just as you are composed of cells with permeable membranes, just as that is your physical structure, so too is it your emotional and spiritual structure. It is also the world's structure. Each of your cells is one of billions within an organism which itself is one of billions as part of a larger cell — the body, mind and spirit you now call "Mark[1]." Mark is also a construct, no more solely Mark than a single blood cell exists apart from the rest of your body. There is an interdependence and interconnectedness without which the organism could not survive. So it is with the construct you call "Mark." So it is with your world. So it is with all the world.

Where are these words coming from? Who are you? What are you?

You have answered that question every day in these writings. If

---

[1] In Penetanguishene I was still Mark, a name I would shed in the months after, following a powerful meditation; I would reclaim it eight years later, along with my middle name, to become the Mark David I am today.

all is one, and it is, then I am you. I am also God in all its guises and definitions. I am energies and entities living and dead, past, present and future. I am each of those and all of those, all at the same time. I am universal consciousness, of which you are a part and a whole, also at the same time. I am the love that you are and all love. I am your divinity and all divinity. I am your wisest self and all wisdom. I am these words and all words. I am the pen that writes these words, the hand that holds the pen and the heart the guides it. There is nothing I am not, which means, once again, that I am you.

This isn't channeling, then. Or is it?

How can you be "channeling" something outside of you when all resides within you? You are not conversing here with something that is separate from the being who holds the pen, the being who sets these words to the page, the being who calls himself Mark. You cannot be if there is no separation, if everything is one. Nor are you delusionally talking to yourself. Rather, you are talking to your Self, that indwelling God Essence/Infinite Intelligence/Heart Mind that will open you to the limitless wisdom of the universe, if you open to it — an "it" that can only be you in a universe where all is and ever will be One.

That's a mind-bender! What pops into my mind from that last bit is the three musketeers' motto: "All for one and one for all."

It is not exactly the same, but it is true, nonetheless. If we are all connected — and we are, inextricably — then we cannot help but act for all when we act for ourselves. That can be constructive or it can be destructive. By healing yourself of your emotional addictions, you act not only for yourself but for the world. For all. By running and hiding in fear, you force the world to run and hide too. Everyone is affected by your every action, by your every thought, by your healing, by your fear. How could it not be? Each cell in your body affects every other. This is no different.

What do I do with this information?

> Take it in. Learn from it. Meditate on it. Communicate it. Inspire with it. Be a missionary with it.

Missionary? That's a loaded word.

> Be an emissary, then. An emissary of light, wisdom and truth. You are here at this time, as are so many others, to spread the light and truth of oneness. That is your work. That is your calling. That is your life.

Writing all this, I feel like a cheap Neale Donald Walsch[2] knockoff.

> Many emissaries are needed to heal the consciousness of the world. Many are called. Each brings unique strengths. Your words — your way — will reach people in ways others cannot.
>
> Don't try to fit in. Don't compare. Don't judge. Your truth is a torch that shines brightly with a flame all its own. Not more brightly than anyone else's, not higher than anyone else's. Nor more dimly nor lower. Yours shines. Theirs shine. None better. None worse. Just is.
>
> Obey your soul's calling. Heed your soul mission. Carry that light, that torch, into the world your way and you will light a path brilliant with spiritual illumination, sparkling with enlightenment.
>
> No one has a monopoly on the expression of truth. Nor is truth ever hidden. It is present within full view for those who choose to let their eyes see, their ears hear, their hearts feel and know. It lies within you and within all, a potential waiting to be acknowledged, accessed, experienced and expressed.

I'm feeling skeptical. Am I making all this up? Is what I'm experiencing here real? Are these dialogues real?

> Is anything real? Is the pen that moves your hand in this moment

---

[2] I had only recently become aware of Walsch's *Conversations with God* but had not yet read it.

real? Is the floor beneath your feet real? Your reality is what you choose it to be, as you have been reminded in recent days. Choose to believe, choose to trust, and it is as real as you allow it to be. Choose to dismiss— Well, you won't, will you?

No. No, I won't. In my heart I know this is real...although I'm starting to not be sure just what "real" is anymore.

Good! That is a beginning.

All this feels radical...almost dangerous...too dangerous...like I could be crucified for talking and writing about it. Is it that dangerous?

Yes and no and it does not matter and cannot matter. There is no life. There is no death. There is only continuity: the oneness of continuity and the continuity of oneness. All else is illusion. You will do, write and say what you must. As will others. That is part of the truth. That is part of the learning. That is part of the healing.

Thank you.

Go, now. Go in truth. Go in light. Go in love. Walk the earth with courage, strength and power. You belong. You matter. You are part of the ground your feet touch. You are one with it. Remember that. And remember love.

Again, thank you.

Namaste.

Friday, January 10, 1997

MORNING

Even before I leave Nova Scotia, I feel called to take my teaching beyond creative writing and into the realm of conscious living, or what I call "creative living." I see a "Pathlights" center as the linchpin of that vision, a vision still barely realized three months into my time in Penetanguishene.

My morning routine includes two affirmations crafted to help me dissolve some of my resistance around writing: "I am more creative every day" and "I write more freely every day."

Once again I feel the need to write. There is no resistance, no feeling of obligation. It's a good feeling, even a comforting one — although it's also disorienting. The need to write what? All I have is a blank page and the inchoate need and desire (hallelujah!) to fill it.

> Trust the emptiness. Trust that out of the emptiness something will emerge.

I willingly choose the dark and enter into the Great Mystery of Life.

> Which is also the Great Mystery of Creation. They are one. Just as dark and light are one, as day and night are one. There is no separation.

I don't mean to be ungrateful, but this talk of oneness is looking to be a repeat of yesterday.

> Perhaps you need to hear it again? Perhaps the words and concepts have yet to be integrated and assimilated into the oneness that is you?

I guess I'm impatient. I want more without having digested what I already have.

> Patience.

I suppose that patience also applies to *The MoonQuest*? I had half-hoped that that's where today's writing would take me.

> Half-hoped: Is that enough? And half-feared?

I suppose. Not enough hope. Too much fear.

> Neither too little nor too much. Just is. All will come as you open yourself to it. Again, remember Nova Scotia. You created that reality, that velocity. Your thoughts and actions created that acceleration, that speed, that possibility. Apply those same positive feelings, thoughts and deeds to what lies ahead and the same result will accrue. That is a law of the universe.

It was easier then, in one sense. There was a concrete outcome I could work toward: a new life in Nova Scotia. It seemed so simple, an answer to my prayers. It was, of course, but not in the way I had expected.

> Ah, expectations… Have you no concrete outcomes in mind and heart now?

I want to finish *The MoonQuest*. I want it to be out there where it can affect others than myself.

> And?

I want my healing work out there, so it can affect others than myself.

> Do you want these more than you fear them?

Some moments yes. Some, no.

> Fear corrodes love. Cancel your fear. Dissolve it.

I can't just snap my fingers and make it vanish…

Can you not? Try it.

I snap my fingers.

Now what?

> Trust. Believe. Desire. Act as though it is possible. Isn't that what you did with Nova Scotia? You acted as though it were possible. You believed in the vision. Doing so brought it into reality. You made it happen, in your God-self omnipotence. You created a reality for yourself that you both needed and desired. Do you have visions for your current dreams?

Not as detailed as those that led to Nova Scotia.

> No matter. That vision was a tool to set you on your way. Its objective truth was less important than its inherent truth. Tell us about your visions.

Are those the same as intuitions?

> For these purposes, yes.

Visions around *The MoonQuest* are murky at best.

> Then begin to clarify them, to flesh them out, to give them substance. Do you believe you can finish it and get it published?

I believe the latter (some days) more than the former.

> And the latter is not possible without the former.

It feels some days as though I'm destined — doomed? — to be writing this book forever.

> If you believe it strongly enough, it will be so. Will it otherwise and it will happen otherwise.

I'm not sure I know how.

> By changing your thoughts and thought patterns. It is more

important to begin there than with action. Thought leads to action. Action predicated on wrong thought leads nowhere.

What can I do?

Your affirmations about writing and creating more freely each day were a start. They helped make this writing possible. See how easily you write these words today? You begin to see what is possible. You trust, and the words flow both through you and from you — the only way they can come when all is one.

Why are the parables and tales in *The MoonQuest* so much easier to write than the main narrative?

You know the answer.

Because only in those do I truly let go, do I truly trust?

You got it.

It's also easier because they are self-contained.

So is each scene within the book, though all is interconnected — the parables as well as the narrative. Do you remember yesterday's words about oneness and interconnectedness? It is the same with your book — our book. Each word, sentence, scene, story-within-the-story is a cell that serves the whole organism. Each needs the other. There is no separateness, no separation. Every action, every thought — both within and without — has its effect, positive or negative.

Our book?

All is one. You are co-creator — not only with that which you believe to be God (which is at the same time you) but with all that is God, which is All, including you.

So what do I need to do? How do I go about it? How do I make the book happen?

First, there is no "making" it happen. There is "letting" it happen. How? Believe in it. Play with it. Rejoice in it. Don't take it so seriously. Begin with these in your thoughts. Move to action only when action is not colored by fear and guilt. Let thoughts move action. Not the other way around.

Of itself, *The MoonQuest* does not matter. Nor does Pathlights. What matters is your heart's desire. What matters is your soul's desire, your soul's light. Follow that light and you will always speak, write and act true and in truth. There are infinite ways to follow that light. *The MoonQuest* and Pathlights are but two. They are the two that at this time you have felt called to follow. They are as good as any others. They are as hard or easy as any others, for you should know by now that "hard" and "easy" are constructs of your own limited mind. Heart and soul are unlimited. Mind has certain restrictions and comes with certain finite boundaries that you must learn to transcend if you are to follow your heart.

Now, tell me about Pathlights. Put your vision into words, however tentative, however unformed. Describe what you know, what you intuit, what you feel. Express what it is you desire.

It's easiest to start there, with what I feel.

As it should be: from feeling to thought to action.

It's about taking what I have learned and continue to learn on my own path and using it to help others along theirs — as guide and teacher and inspiration. I see taking my words — *The MoonQuest* and other writing and speaking — out into the world. You used the word "missionary" yesterday. Perhaps I bridled because that's how I see myself, but in what I like to think is a more enlightened sense of the word: carrying the words of my heart to people of free will, offering them my wisdom and experience and letting them make their own choices, letting them choose their own path.

A noble ideal.

Ideal? You mean it's not possible?

> It is as possible as you believe it to be. Start by believing it possible and before you know it, it will be here, even if it does not show up precisely as you envision it in this moment. Regardless, the spirit and essence of it will be true to your vision.
>
> It can happen. And it can happen without struggle. You see too much as struggle, too much as work. You believe you do not deserve unless you have suffered, and even then you are not altogether convinced. These dialogues are the result of trust and surrender, not struggle. Apply trust and surrender to everything else in your life and you and your "work" will take off and soar beyond your wildest imaginings.

And then I'll be shot down.

> There is no death. Only continuity. Follow your heart, your soul's mission, and no true harm can come to you. Why do you still fear annihilation when annihilation is not possible? Whatever has happened to you before, in this life or another, you are still here, stronger and more powerful — more empowered — than ever.

There is a little boy in me who finds that hard to believe.

> Take that boy in your arms. Rock him in a gentle, enfolding, protective embrace. Croon to him a lullaby. Sing to him of your strength, and his. Sing to him of your power, and his. Sing to him of oneness, interconnectedness, limitlessness. Sing to him of interdependence. Sing to him of healing and wholeness. Sing to him of life. Most important of all, sing to him of love.
>
> Love heals all wounds, all doubts, all fears. Love frees up the possibility in everything. So, you see, your dreams are possible. Your very presence — here, at this moment in this place, inner and outer — is testament to that. Trust love as you trust these words that once you would have scoffingly fled from. You scoff no longer.

Know that mountains can be moved with the power of a single thought. Your power is limitless. Embrace it. Love it. Exercise it — for good, for God, for life, for love. Dream. Envision. Believe. Change your thoughts. Be conscious. Be aware.

Why resist? You will come around in the end, so you might as well come around now — to your heart, to your soul. To your mission. Yes, you are a missionary. For what else is a soul with a mission? Respect that mission. Trust it and surrender to it. Open your heart and mind to it. Do that and anything is possible. Do that and there are no limits save those you create through fear or unbelief. All is possible. All is connected. All is one.

Thank you.

Namaste.

Saturday, January 11, 1997
MORNING

I awake to a vague dream memory of volcanic eruptions, recalling little but the explosive power of a fiery lava flow that harms no one.

There's a lot of nattering and chattering going on in my head this morning. Lots of accusation. Lots of uncertainty. Lots of doubt. How do I silence it?

> Be still, and know that I am God, that you are God, that all around you is God, that nothing is not-God, including your nattering and chattering. Do not beat yourself up for the nattering and chattering. Do not beat yourself up for the doubt and uncertainty. Do not beat yourself up for beating yourself up. Let the thoughts, whatever they are, come. Let the thoughts, whatever they are, go. Don't fight them. Let them have their say and they will let you have the stillness and peace you seek. Remember that all your feelings and emotions, including those you would prefer not to experience, are part of your humanity, part of your growth.

Then I must be having a growth spurt.

> Indeed you are. You learn and grow every minute of every hour of every day, whether or not you are conscious of it. Much of the time— No, *most of the time*. That was the initial wording but you censored it. In censoring these words you censor only yourself. In diminishing these words you diminish only yourself.
>
> Recognize your power, the power of your words. Acknowledge it. Embrace it. Live it. No one will destroy you for it. There is no annihilation, as you have already written here. There cannot be

when all is one. You may tire of hearing these words but until you believe them more fully, until you live them more fully, they cannot bear too much repeating. Say it.

All is one.

There is more. Say what is in your heart.

I can't seem to touch that place this morning. All I can touch is fear and powerlessness.

That is not true and you know it.

Saying it makes it so.

Then un-say it. Reclaim your power as you did on your morning walk. Reclaim your power and flush your fear into Mother Earth, where it can be composted and transformed into affirmative energy. Ground yourself.

I joyously reclaim my power and lovingly let go of all that holds me back.

There is more.

God is all and all is God. All is oneness. There is no separation. I am one with all and all is one with me.

Do you believe that?

Saying it doesn't make it so.

You cannot have it both ways.

So I'm inconsistent.

You are inconsistent when it upholds your perceived powerlessness. You use consistency to that same end. That is not only counterproductive, it is destructive, self-destructive.

My hand hurts. I want to stop.

> Surrender to your wisest self, your most powerful self. Surrender to your oneness, to your unity, to your divinity. Surrender to your words. Surrender now or surrender later, for you will surrender. To borrow from your popular culture, resistance is futile.

Cute. Seriously, why was there such a shift in me today? The week was going so well. What happened?

> Fear happened. Fear tangled and ensnared you. It happens. Yet you need not stay tangled and ensnared. You can dissolve those knots of fear with an act of will. Your will: It won't. It can't. Just say: "That's fear. Okay, I acknowledge it. But I will not be afraid. I am stronger than it is, more powerful than it is. Bigger than it is."

When I try that it has no impact.

> Not immediately discernible. But like a vaccination, each time builds up your immunity for the next. So say it, even if nothing seems to shift. Each time you think it, say it, write it, it makes a difference. That difference will show up — ultimately.

I don't want to deny my feelings. I have done too much of that.

> That is why you must first acknowledge your feelings of fear. Only then can you cancel and dissolve them. You cannot move through and past what you refuse to acknowledge.
>
> You already do this much of the time, just as you already act from a place of consciousness most of the time, just as you are more fearless and more conscious than most a lot of the time. Just as you let yourself be more vulnerable in the world than most, nearly always. That is what makes you a good teacher, guide and inspiration.

It feels like a burden sometimes, like if I could just lapse into unconsciousness for a bit, everything would be easier.

> Of the moment only. You would be profoundly dissatisfied.

I know. Which is why I persevere.

That is a strong word, a loaded word, a word redolent of struggle and unhappiness.

I saw it as I was writing it. It's the word "severe" embedded within it.

You see? You are conscious! Carry that conscious awareness into more elements of your life. Notice what you do, what you say, what you think, what you imagine. These are what create your reality. Begin to alter them and your reality will begin to shift too.

I can't help but feel there's some dishonesty there.

This is not to suggest that you deny your feelings, that you deny your fear. Instead of "I'm not frightened," how about "I acknowledge my fear, love it and let it go."

That works better for me. Thank you. I wouldn't have thought of that on my own.

But you did.

But—

There is no separation between the two "sides" of these dialogues. All is one.

Right. Now what?

Have you had enough?

Parts of me had enough before we started. Parts of me hunger for more.

Which parts are in ascendancy right now?

The hungry parts.

Good. What would you like to know?

What about this volcano, from last night's dream?

> What about it? You know what it is.

My power?

> Your nascent power, getting ready to erupt, to explode, to spread its light into the heavens, to thunder its message to the far corners of the universe, to let its molten lava run into the earth, feed the earth — just as it was fed from the earth. You noticed that the volcano harmed no one?

I did.

> So will your power, wisely exercised, harm no one. Wisely exercised, it can do nothing but heal, but cast light into the darkness. You will change the world, as all who are conscious change the world.
>
> Now, go on with your day. Enter into it consciously, aware of each step, each thought, each mood, each word, each action. Open your awareness and you can begin to change your reality. Then you will begin to find abundance in all spheres.

Thank you for these words, this wisdom.

> This wisdom is available to all who open their hearts. So it is, of course, available to you. Thank yourself for opening your heart, for having the courage to open your heart. Whatever these words seem to have done for you, *you* have done. You are reluctant to acknowledge that. Do not be. This is not an "ego thing," as you would put it. It is an "empowerment thing." It is an acknowledgment of your role in your own life. Until you acknowledge that, you cannot alter your reality. Because until you acknowledge it, you do not believe in your own power. Believe in it, for your power is indeed great. It is limited only by your belief in limitation. Dissolve that and anything is truly possible. So, thank yourself.

I understand what you're saying. It just feels awkward. The language doesn't seem to support it.

Language, as you often tell your clients and students, is only an approximation. It can never capture the totality of experience, which is limitless and ultimately beyond description. But it is the only tool you have.

How about this? I acknowledge my power over my life and reality. And I will the changes that will lead me to wholeness.

Wonderful. Now, go in love, peace, healing and empowerment. Go, carry your volcanic fire out into the world. Go, and make a difference.

I will it so.

So be it. Namaste.

Sunday, January 12, 1997

MORNING

Two dreams hang suspended in my consciousness as I sit down to write. In one, I try to control Roxy, who tugs and tugs and tugs until she breaks free of the lock on her retractable leash. In the other, I dance with carefree abandon — twirling, spinning and flying in all directions to something called both "Waltz of the Boardwalk" and "Marche de la Promenade." As I touch pen to paper, the music still playing in my head, a story emerges. Once again, I hope it will be for The MoonQuest, *where such parable-like fables play an integral role. Once again, my judgment threatens to abort my efforts. (This is more trialogue than dialogue, with the story adding its own voice and font.)*

Once upon a time there was a king.

Another king?

Another king. Only this king was different.

    They are always different.

If they're always different, I can have any king I want.

    Touché!

Once upon a time there was a king who lost his kingdom. He woke up one morning and it was gone. Vanished.

This is starting to sound familiar, like a story that's already in *The MoonQuest*.

    Wait. Don't prejudge.

Where there had once been a castle, stood ruins: half walls of crumbling stone, floors of grass where slate and marble had once lain. It was perhaps as well, for the king woke up on what had once been the floor. And although the grasses were not downy as his feather mattress had been, they were far softer and warmer than hard slate or cold marble. No four-poster canopy protected him. No roof protected him. In fact, his first sight, upon opening his eyes, was the gray-pink-plum of dawn. And his first sensation was of damp. The dew had settled indiscriminately, over him as well as over the land. The dew was sweet and cool, jewels of watery light that perched almost weightlessly upon every surface, twinkling and winking in this first, tentative ray of sunshine.

I've lost it.

> You haven't. The story is there. Trust it. Trust yourself. Close your eyes and trust.

I'm afraid to close my eyes.

> Why?

Afraid of what I'll see.

> Dissolve your fear. Will it away. Ground yourself in the story. Be one with the story.

The king, too, was afraid. He looked past the ruins of his once-mighty fortress and saw nothing he recognized: no roads, no farms, no villages. Had they ever existed, the land had now conquered them. Fields of wildflowers stretched far beyond the castle walls, a crabbed apple tree in full spring bloom, the only—

I can't. I don't know where this is taking me. I don't know how to let it take me there. I can't maintain my concentration, my focus. I want it come easily.

> Let it go, and it will come. Don't force it. Surrender to the story.

I thought this was supposed to be easy.

> There is no "supposed to be." There is just what is. Close your eyes. Whenever you are stuck, close your eyes, breathe and

reconnect with the power that is yours, the power that is the story.

Fields of wildflowers stretched beyond the castle walls — purple, yellow, indigo, violet, crimson, ocher — a velvety carpet that was broken only by a crabbed apple tree in full spring bloom and by a boulder of pink-and-gray granite that rose in smooth contours higher than any man. Beyond the flowering meadow stood a deep, dense forest, barely clothed with bright green buds and the first unfolding of new leaf. Were it not for the familiar layout of this castle ruin — rooms, halls and corridors all seemed to be where they belonged, as best he could tell from the knee-high floor plan that remained of them — he would believe himself in some foreign land. Instead, he seemed to be in some foreign time far into the future when his kingdom had ceased to be.

How could it simply vanish, this kingdom that he and generations before him had fought for so valiantly? Yet it had. And his kingship along with it, for when he rose, he wore no royal nightclothes, nor royal clothes of any sort. Instead, he wore sturdy traveling gear, of a heavy enough weave that the morning dew had not soaked through.

The king woke hungry, but there was no bell pull by what had once been his bed. Even had there been, no servant would have responded, and no cook would have prepared a morning repast. No servants. No cook. No one.

He cast his eyes from horizon to horizon. All he saw was wild, overgrown, with sign of neither habitation nor habitant. Wherever he was, whatever place or time this was, he was alone.

He thought at first of laying back down, closing his eyes and trusting that when he woke from the ensuing sleep all would be restored. He thought it and dismissed it.

"I did not become a king by running from the unknown," he declared. Yet he was afraid. The unknown surrounded him and, despite its openness, pressed in on him. But he would not run. He stood now, and as the suns rose full and bright from their own sleeping places, he began to explore.

He started with the castle, following its crumbling walls from room to room. He knew this place, had designed it and had supervised its construction. Here was the throne room. Here was the dining hall and here, the kitchens. Here was the library. All those volumes, some hundreds of years old. What had become of them? And what had become of the furnishings and tapestries, the jewels and treasures?

When he reached the ballroom he though he caught the faint trace of a waltz and thought he saw flickers of brightly colored fabric spinning and twirling in time. He began to hum along: DUM-dee-dee, DUM-dee-dee, DUM-dee-dee.

Yet as soon as the sound crossed his lips the ghostly accompaniment ceased. Had it been the breeze riffling the grasses in three-four time? Or had he stepped for an instant back to that other time where all was as it had been? He shook his head free of sound and memory and moved out beyond the castle perimeter.

Where a broad, deep moat had once encircled the impregnable outer wall, a tiny stream trickled over a scattering of rocks, emptying into a spring. No, it bubbled up from the spring — burbled and bubbled like a kettle on the boil.

This isn't going anywhere. Why isn't this going anywhere?

Must it?

Oughtn't it? I'm hungry and confused.

So was the king...

"I'm hungry and confused," the king confessed to the spring. He cupped his hands into its coolness, splashed some water on his face and then drank deeply from its sweetness. He patted his pockets and found a hunk of dew-damp bread and a slab of cheese and devoured them greedily. In another pocket he found a hunting knife and a ball of twine. In another, he found a map.

A map! Excitedly, he unfolded the canvas upon which it was drawn, expecting to find some clue to his whereabouts. But when he smoothed it on the ground and pressed his face close to the faded ink, he groaned in disappointment. The representation was of no place he recognized and the words were formed of characters totally foreign, though he knew many languages. Turn it which way he would, it divulged none of its secrets.

"Where am I?" he cried into the spring.
"You are home," it seemed to reply.
"Where is that?"

"Where you are."

Angry with frustration, he clawed a rock from the ground and heaved it into the waters. As it struck the surface it threw up a curtain of water that hung there in midair, blocking all from the king's vision.

Can I stop now?

Why? You're just getting to the good part! You know you will feel terrible if you just leave this.

Yes, but I'm frustrated.

Stick with it, a bit longer.

When the water cleared what seemed like hours later but was only an instant, the scene had shifted. Castle ruins, meadow and forest had vanished. Now there was nothing, only light. The king seemed to be perched on a giant water droplet, staring into a nothingness of brilliant light. "Or," he wondered in a moment of horror, "have I shrunk to such a size that I now fit atop a water droplet?"

The droplet rose, bubbling up higher and higher, past other prism-like drops. The king felt as though he were within a rainbow, arching across the sky, being carried heavenward and down again. The bubble bobbed and swayed as it rose, lulling the king into a doze, then into a deep sleep.

When he awoke, in his own bed, in his own castle, in his own land, he knew he had dreamed but that it had been no dream. He knew that the land of his dream, where all was past, present and future as one, had been as real as this place. And he knew that he had visited there before without having remembered. The gift was in the memory restored. The gift was in the acknowledgment of other realities that lay parallel to his own. The gift was in not having run in fear back to sleep, as perhaps he had done before, but in letting the dream carry him where it would, regardless of where it was, regardless of the meaning it might or might not have. The gift was in surrender.

He had not been a bad king until that point. But nor had he been a particularly wise one. Without knowing it from moment to moment, he grew wise and good. And although he never revisited that other place again, he visited others, yet more strange and confounding, though in each one the Waltz of the Boardwalk wafted gently on the breeze, reminding him who he was and where he had come from.

He ruled for many more years and when he died, a very old man, he knew more than he could have ever imagined. He died happy and content, ready now to return to those lands he had visited only in dream.

What was that all about?

> Trust and surrender. Yours, not the king's. The story does not matter. Your stress was in wanting to make it matter, in assuming it had to be part of *The MoonQuest* and trying to control it even as you let it come. You must not control.

Yes. Last night's dream about Roxy suggested that I was still trying to control too much that needs to be instinctual.

> This experience with your story confirms that. Make no assumptions. Have no expectations. Just let go in surrender. Nothing else is asked of you. And once you achieve surrender, everything is given to you.
>
> You have come a long way. This is a means of showing you not to be complacent. There remains a distance to go. Not a discouraging distance. But you must remember to be conscious, to be aware, to surrender. That is the key, to All.

Is that all? Can I go now?

> You are angry.

No. Yes. I don't know. This dialogue has not been as "divine" as others, and the story not as clear as others.

> You create your own reality.

I know. I want to leave this feeling uplifted. But I don't.

> Sit quietly, not in reflection, but in emptiness. Let the void wash over you. Welcome the void. Befriend it. Embrace it. Love it. Now, close your eyes and let the rainbow carry you where it will.

Not where I will.

> Precisely.

I sit in meditative silence for a time...

That helped. It didn't cure, but it helped. I'm aware that my emotions are much closer to the surface on an empty, gnawing stomach. And I'm aware that I'm now more able to watch my thoughts and cancel them. The first temptation is always to stop them in a brutal way. I'm beginning to learn to be gentler, more compassionate about it. It's hard.

> No one said it would be easy. But you are doing fine. You have done good work today. Now, go play.

It's that old "I'll try." It keeps wanting to surface. I will myself to not try but to be, to try to — I did it again! — to recapture the joyful abandonment I felt as I danced to the music of my dream. I realized, in meditation, that both "promenade" and "boardwalk" speak to a path, to a path that I dance to.

> Nice.

Yeah, I thought so!

> Go, now. Go dance with joy. Dance your dance of light, love and laughter, your dance of exultation and surrender.

I will it so.

> So be it. Namaste.

Tuesday, January 14, 1997
3:00 A.M.

I wake up in the middle of the night, several hours after receiving both a powerful shiatsu/energy treatment from a local practitioner and a phone call from a friend seeking a loan. Each experiences stirs up old emotions, old patterns of behavior and old fears of judgment and rejection.

No dreams at this hour, at least none remembered; just more nattering and chattering voices, this time in response to Michael's most powerful healing session. They are afraid, these voices — of change. They are angry, these voices, because their status quo is being attacked. It's too late for them. The status quo that they try to preserve is already the status quo ante. The changes they fear are already in process and cannot be reversed. Toxins leap over each other to flee my body, suddenly an inhospitable environment after all these years. "Good riddance," I say. Yet all this feverish inner activity has left me feeling...feverish. And last night's late dinner, light though it was, sits awkwardly within.

Heat woke me up, a suffocating, stifling heat that didn't quite vanish, only diminished, when I got out of bed for water and a digestive enzyme. I'm tired, so very tired. I'm tired of resisting, tired of living half-lives. I crave peace. Not the peace of death but of resolution. I crave oneness, unity, lack of separation. I crave it and will have it. I will it so — despite the voices, despite the fear, despite the discomfort, which is merely resistance to the inevitable surrender.

The end is coming and with it a new beginning...a new dawn...a new day...and an ancient, timeless power. Hail to it and to my place in the universe, to my healing and wholeness, to my journey and sacred path. Hail and truth. Truth and the voice to speak it. Truth and the balls to live it. Truth and the light to make it known and seen. And manifest.

AFTERNOON

I open my eyes from a nap feeling out-of-sorts, weighed down by a half-promise to spend time with Jeremy Emery and by my guilty reluctance to tell him about my nontraditional spiritual path. The result? Sharp gas pains that yoga stretches, ginger tea and other digestive remedies fail to soothe. I turn to a more potent cure: the blank page.

Why am I in such a state?

> Why do you think?

All this change coming so quickly…all these old patterns that I feel called to jettison…all these emotions that I don't know what to do with…it feels overwhelming. It *is* overwhelming.

> You are powerful beyond measure. Powerful beyond imagining. Everything you need to move through this — all the strength, all the courage, all the tools, inner and outer — are there, present, available for you.

But there's so much.

> This is nothing. A blip.

Not for me.

> Even for you. You carry the God-energy within. Don't hold it in reserve. Exercise it. Call on it. That is why it resides in you.

But what do I *do*!?

> "Doing" again, when "being" is all that is called for. Being and trust.

I trust. I trusted enough to book that energy session. I trusted enough to handle Lorraine's loan request in a way I never would have in the past. But I'm afraid. Afraid of these uncharted waters of belief I'm being thrown into. What will people think of me? How will I speak my truth when my truth is so alien, so outlandish?

> You will speak and write what you know in your heart to be true. That will be your shield. That will be your armor. That will be your protection. There is no other. There is no hiding. The stakes are too high.

That places too heavy a burden on my shoulders.

> Your shoulders are broad enough, broad enough to carry more weight still — as long as you bear it lightly and lightheartedly. This is about truth. Carrying your truth. Communicating your truth. Speaking and writing your truth. Being your truth.

I want to move into my truth. I want to heal and be healed. I want to be in your— in *my* power, to fulfill my destiny, to be what I was born to be. Yet at this moment it feels overwhelming. I don't know how to communicate all this. I can't even communicate it to Jeremy.

> Don't beat yourself up for not being able to share your path fully, coherently — especially with a nine-year-old boy. This is still raw for you, strange for you, nascent within you. Give yourself time. You *are* speaking out. You are writing — these words, for example. You will do even more as the newness wears away and the naturalness takes over. It will become second-nature, as so much else that you once feared has become.
>
> You have acknowledged your present fear. Now let it dissolve. Feel the earth beneath you, supporting you, grounding you. Breathe in the power of the earth. Stop and breathe. Feel the power of your being as it merges with the earth, as the earth energy and your energy become one, the one they have been all along. Feel your power being awakened, being opened up, being healed. You are strong. You are strength itself. Feel it.

I feel a tingling in my groin.

> That is your power being awakened, being opened up. Feel the awakening power of your masculinity. Open your heart and mind to it. Be it.

It's strange and wonderful and scary all at the same time.

> Stay connected with that earth power, the power that stretches down to the molten core, that connects the earth's core with yours. A direct line: heart to heart, core to core. You are that direct line — one with the earth, one with all. One with the energy that is everywhere, that is all things, that is everything. Take a moment to do that.

I sit for a moment in meditative silence, letting myself feel my connection with the earth.

> Now that you are linked to the earth, let the light from the heavens rain down on you. Let this white light flow into you, suffuse you with lightness, with the mystery that is all things and no-thing. Let it. Breathe it in now.

I do that too.

> Now, take those two energies, heaven and earth, and let them braid within you to form an energy of pure truth and pure unity, a unity that merges with the unity of you to form a oneness that transcends all fear, all disbelief, all distrust. It is holy union, holy communion, the all-embracing unity that is all-life.
>
> From that unity, draw your strength, your faith and your love. There, you will find the Divine...the Divine that is you. Sit with it. Surrender to it. Let it melt away your fear, your feelings of inadequacy, your feelings of danger. For within this unity is the only safety.

Then I'm doomed.

> Nonsense. You know that not to be true. Even in your fear, you

know that not to be true. Your fear is diminishing, is it not?

Diminishing but not vanishing.

Sit quietly and will those outdated beliefs to dissolve. Let go your skepticism. Let go your ego-need to work and suffer. Let in ease and lightness. Let in love. Surrender into that oneness that is all and that is nothing, which is all part the Great Mystery of Life. Enter into that mystery. Enter into it, embrace it and become one with it. It is your sword and your shield. It is your tool of healing and wholeness. It is the key to all and the source of all — of all that is you and beyond you, which are, ultimately, one.

You are safer now, here in your truth, than ever before. All will be well if you will it so. You can do it. You must do it. Do you?

I will.

Louder.

I will it so.

Say it and believe it.

I WILL IT SO.

Now, sit in the stillness of that and be it.

Wednesday, January 15, 1997
LATE EVENING

In the meditation that precedes this dialogue, a giant, pearl-gray eagle named Tikor, with me on his back enfolded in an orb of white light, soars up and past the moon and stars. "I carry you through the dark and into the light," he tells me, adding that the orb of light is my heart when it is fully open. He tells me not to be afraid, to trust. He tells me that faith is my fortress, love is my shield and truth is my armor. He tells me I will soon fly on my own power. "Oh, how you will fly," he exclaims. "The places you will see. The world is only now beginning to open up for you and to you. Let it explode in a firmament of light and color. Show that radiance to the world. The world needs all that is birthing within you."

Thank you, for all the gifts of this meditation.

> Inhale the gifts. Integrate and assimilate them. They are already one with your heart, mind and body — if you will it. Do you?

I do.

> Speak it.

I will my truth to be manifest — to be visible to my own heart and eyes and to the world.

> Whatever the cost?

Whatever the cost.

> Then thy will be done.

So be it.

> So be it. Namaste.

Thursday, January 16, 1997

NOON

I feel much fear as this day begins — of the power released by the shiatsu/energy treatment and of the power of the eagle Tikor...power I feel reluctant to embrace as my own. Through it all, I can't stop comparing myself, unfavorably, to Neale Donald Walsch.

> You are neither less than nor greater than anyone, including Neale Donald Walsch. You and these words — all your words — are part of the universal well of creation that all share and that all can access if they choose...if they dare. You have dared.

I have.

> Bravo! You had a realization earlier. Repeat it here. It is important.

It hearkens back to my George and Beth dream[3]: "I must write."

> What followed on that?

"I must be free to write gibberish." I must be free — I must free myself — to let whatever flows from my pen to touch the page. It's what I have taught and it's what I have done my best to live. It's time now to put it more fully into practice.

> What strength you now speak with. Can you take the strength of this moment and apply it in every moment, to all your creations?

Translating it to *The MoonQuest* feels more difficult.

> Then don't set out to do that right now. Set out to write — freely and openly. Set out to dialogue and let these dialogues carry you

---

3 See November 26 entry.

where they will. They may even carry you back to *The MoonQuest*. Or not. It does not matter. It cannot matter. Only the moment matters. Others' opinions don't matter. Your own judgment does not matter. *Now* matters. Make now matter by living it, by being true to it, by honoring and respecting it — as you do some of the time. You edit and censor these words again!

I couldn't bring myself to write "much of the time." Why?

Why do you think?

I can't acknowledge my own strength and power, my own progress.

Acknowledge how far you have come in such a short time. Acknowledge it, take it in and let yourself recognize that the distance left for you to travel is shorter than you think.

I fear that the distance is still too long. Even more, I fear that the distance barely exists. I think that's what this morning's fear has been about: a reaction to yesterday's feeling of—

Power?

Yes.

And clarity?

Yes.

Embrace those. They are the truth of who you truly are. Do you want that truth expressed through *The MoonQuest* and Pathlights?

Yes.

How is it going to happen?

By me making — no, *letting* it happen.

Yes, not forcing. Not passive either. Actively let it happen. Support that "letting" with your thoughts, inspirations, words and actions. Yesterday with Tikor was a start. Believe in the reality of your dreams. Will them to happen, and they will. Perhaps, like Nova Scotia, not in the precise form you expect. But they will manifest. Trust, and it will be so.

What now?

> What do you want to do?

I don't know.

> Yes, you do.

Write?

> Why not?

Write what?

> Anything. Gibberish. Dialogue. Whatever. Sit in stillness and meditate. See/feel/experience what emerges. Are you up for that?

Do I have a choice?

> You always have a choice.

Yeah, between being and not-being.

> That is a choice.

I may procrastinate. I may try to defer.

> Dissolve those thoughts. Try "I will."

I will?

> Without the question mark.

I will. I will set pen to paper and — oh, that "try to" keeps trying to come out — and see where it takes me.

> And...

And it won't matter if it takes me nowhere at all. That's a harder one.

Of course it is. Hence, its importance. Go now. Go and create.

Thank you.

Namaste.

AFTERNOON

It doesn't matter how freely I have written in recent days. It doesn't matter how fearless I have felt in recent hours. This is a new moment, fraught with fresh anxieties and new fears.

I don't want to be here. I want to eat…to sleep…to run…to hide.

> Yet you do none of those. You are here. You write. You set pen to paper.

More writhing than writing.

> Even so. You are here doing what you feel called to do. For that alone, it is important that you acknowledge your courage and strength.

I feel neither. Just cold and frightened.

> The chill will pass, as will the fear. You have crossed the greatest hurdle: You have listened, trusted and heeded. Even if were you to stop right now, you would have taken a giant leap. But you are not going to stop, are you?

No. Now what?

> Leap again. Leap into the void. Release all expectation. Don't assume another profound dialogue. Don't assume another *MoonQuest* scene. Don't assume a visionary experience. Assume

nothing and enter the Great Mystery willingly. How can it be any kind of mystery if you know its secrets before stepping across the threshold, before stepping through the portal?

My life is coming to an end and I don't know what to do about it.

Nothing. Let it.

Easy to say. I'm afraid of what lies on the other side of this portal you are asking me to cross.

You are asking you to cross.

True. But I want promises. I want guarantees. I want to know I'll be safe.

You know such promises would have no meaning. Parts of you are dying this day of wintry death. So much waits to be born in its place, but it can only be born to the void. It can only be born in trust. It can only be born in surrender. Even as parts of you die, you do not die. The essence that is you cannot die. Truth cannot die, light cannot die, love cannot die, though they can be buried. Whatever happens, your soul always lives on.

These words are very pretty, but they offer no assurances. I want absolute assurances. I want things to continue just as they are.

In fear, pain and paralysis?

Well, not that.

What, then?

I don't know. All I know is that the pain is too great. I want it to stop.

It can and will if you will it so. It can and will if you let go, when you let go. It has happened before. It will happen again.

And again and again and again. Does this never stop?

> Does the cycle of life, death and rebirth ever cease? Look beyond your body. Look at the storm whipping snow against the window. Do you doubt that spring will come even in the midst of all this frozen death?

No, but—

> Do you doubt that the cycle of seasons will continue to move through its dance of birth, life, death, rebirth?

No.

> The same is as true for the you that occupies this body in this moment in human history as it is for the soul that occupies it at this nanosecond in cosmic history. You are here to grow forward. Here in this house, in this town, at this time, in this life. You are learning and you are teaching. All are teachers who live their lives consciously. Who spoke those words last night to Trish to such effect?

I did.

> Does that not tell you anything?

That I'm more powerful than I know, more powerful than I feel I have any right to be. I'm afraid of that power. I'm afraid I'll abuse it, afraid I'll hurt someone, afraid I'll destroy not create, harm not heal— That's new. I didn't know that before. Where does that come from? A past life?

> It does not matter. Other lives do not matter at this moment. Other moments in this life do not matter at this moment. What matters in this moment *is* this moment and what you are prepared to do with it. Are you prepared to live it or run from it?

Part of me wants to run. More of me wants to live it.

> Then live it you shall, if you give yourself permission. Whoever you may have been who once abused power, you are not that

person now. Whoever you may have been who was once the victim of abuse, you are not that person now. You are who you are in this moment: a living, loving, wise soul; a healer, writer and visionary of great power. You are called to exercise and express that power out in the world. Do you dare refuse the call?

You know I don't.

> Then heed your call, as you do already, and miracles will continue to unfold all around you — in your life and in the lives of those yours touches. You believe in miracles, don't you?

My being here is testament to so many miracles. What am I called on to do?

> Live your miracles and as you do, help reawaken miracle-vision in those who have become blind to miracles. Listen. Trust. Surrender. Don't judge yourself so harshly. Let love fill you, pour from you and surround you always — even in the midst of whatever fear you cannot immediately dissolve. Free your faith to create more miracles. Free your faith to create your destiny. Surrender to that destiny. Surrender. Surrender. And surrender yet more.

I do. I surrender. Thank you.

> Namaste.

Friday, January 17, 1997

EVENING

*T*his afternoon, I find myself chatting with the sales clerk at my local art store — sharing with her not only the spiritual journey that brought me to the area but my previous night's dream, a dream so powerful that it is still with me hours later. In the dream, a voice tells me something important; I try but fail to hold the message in my consciousness. Then, a second voice with a second message, which I also fail to retain. Finally, a message I remember: "I will give you one thing only: that you will teach the world how to love and be healthy." When I leave the store, having uncharacteristically revealed something deeply personal to a stranger, I recoil in retroactive fear and panic.

From a long-ago meditation: I stand in the middle of a bridge, unable to continue across for fear of what might await me on the other side. In the midst of my paralysis, I sense an angel floating behind me. She gently guides me across the span as a part of me that refuses to make the journey dissolves into dust.

I'm having a hard time stilling my mind. It wanders all over the place. I want to rein it in. It's so frustrating.

> So you punish yourself.

I guess I do.

>> There is no need. This is not about perfection or control. There is nothing to "rein in" or "reign over." It is about letting — letting the thoughts come through, then letting them go. The more you try to control your thoughts, the more stubbornly they will persist. Remember what you used to say about meditation? That

the mere fact of being able to sit still for five or ten or twenty minutes was of value, even if you couldn't still your mind for but a few of them.

So, accept those thoughts. Welcome them, and once they feel welcome, they will no longer feel the need to attach themselves to you. They will feel able to let go and so will you. Do not judge them. Do not judge yourself. Self-judgment is a no-win game, for you will always find yourself wanting at the end of it, unable to meet some unrealistic standard. Because as high as you stretch and as deep as you grow, that insecure perfectionist part of you will always raise the stakes. By all means, set goals for yourself. Just don't set them unreasonably high, don't cling obsessively to them and don't use them as a whip with which to lash yourself. Let go self-punishment. You are better than that, stronger than that, light-brighter than that.

I'm anxious.

Because you don't know where this is going?

Is that the reason? I don't know. But I feel a tightness in my chest and my nose is all blocked. Plus heartburn.

It will pass. Acknowledge your anxiety and let it go. Dissolve it. You don't have to know what it is about to dissolve it. Just let it go.

Easier said than done.

As easily done as said.

I'm intimidated by the gift of last night's dream.

Accept it as the gift it was, as the opportunity it was. Accept it and let it go. You need not do anything. That is the source of your anxiety, is it not?

Partly. I feel as though there is something I ought to do, something that will make me worthy of the message.

> Listen to your words. They are self-diminishing and controlling. Don't judge. The gift itself is proof of your worthiness. Accept it as offered and share it, as you did today at the art store.

But I just blurted it out. I didn't know what I was doing.

> Of course you did. You listened, trusted and heeded — without understanding, without needing to understand. That is what surrender is all about. That is what these dialogues are all about. That is what your writing is all about. Don't get bogged down in questioning, in analysis. All you need to do is keep your heart open. You did that today. You did well today. Celebrate that.

Then why do I feel so anxious, so tight?

> Because you cannot see what lies ahead. Yet you are not blind. You see much — more than most. That is your gift.

Or my curse.

> Never a curse. Fear it less and value it more. Uncertainty cannot harm you. Doubt can.

Hmm.

> "This isn't good enough. This isn't profound enough. This isn't new enough. This isn't sellable." You don't write those words, but you think them, don't you?

Part of me wants Divine Revelation, wants fireworks and grand pronouncements, wants prophecy.

> You have had all those, even when you have not realized it. You have had them and will continue to have them, as long as you keep your heart open and trust. Trust that you are getting what you need: from your words, from your encounters, from all the gifts, recognized and not, that embrace you every day.

I am grateful…and afraid.

Don't run from your fear. Be your fear. Then be your fearlessness. You stand on the edge, afraid to step forward. Remember your dream experience on the bridge? Eventually, the angel piloted you across and that part of you that could not cross dissolved into dust. It has happened countless times since without your being conscious of it. It will happen again.

I'm tired of the fear, tired of the waiting.

In your fatigue you will let them both go, for the latter is necessitated by the former. Now, sit in stillness, then return to your evening in strength, renewed by this experience and by your own divinity.

Thank you.

Namaste.

Acts

Just as one season must always melt into the next, so my season of retreat was drawing to an end. I had arrived in Penetanguishene with neither agenda nor timetable. Now, my intuition told me, it was time to prepare for my return to Toronto, time to carry the growth I had experienced in solitude back out into the world...time to act.

Sunday, January 19, 1997

EVENING

I feel empowered this evening. I feel strong. I want to keep feeling that feeling. But it feels fragile. I feel fear lurking in the shadows, waiting for a weak moment so it can pounce.

> First, fear is not your enemy. It is your teacher. Everything you feel and experience is your teacher. Next, know that you grow in strength by the minute and that your fearlessness spreads and deepens. You are ready for big things. Big things are ready for you. Feel it within every cell of your being. Feel it, for feeling it makes it so.
>
> Know your power, and don't flee from it or cringe before it, just as it does not serve you to flee from or cringe before your fear. Don't edit or censor yourself. Trust your intuition. Trust your message as you trust these messages.
>
> Clear away the lingering residues of the past that tie you down, that keep you from flying on the broad wings of the eagle. Cut loose the bonds that constrict and restrict you. Slice through the chains that still enslave you. Only you can free yourself. Only you can free yourself to help free others.
>
> You worry about the words, about the vehicles, you will use to help others. Don't. All you need will be provided. Remain open and as you might say, "Stay tuned."

Film at 11?

> You never know. Now, rest. Rest to ready yourself for the wondrous opportunities and experiences that await you. Just believe that you deserve them. Ready yourself, too, for love, for intimacy, for the blossoming and explosion of your sexuality

— not long overdue, as you are thinking, but right on time. It is all right on time, just when you are ready to make the most of it.

Thank you. This has been yet another amazing gift.

One of many to come. And it comes because you open your heart to it and to your wisest self, to your divinity. It has always been present, waiting for you to be ready for it, to desire it, to surrender to it, to know that you deserve it. It has waited for you as it waits for all — patiently, without judgment and in infinite love.

Thank you.

Thank you, and namaste.

Monday, January 20, 1997

MORNING

I wake up this wintry morning afraid that it's a repeat of another winter morning — three years and eleven hundred miles in the past when I realized that my obsessive journaling had absorbed all my writing energy and was preventing me from getting back to The MoonQuest, *set aside five months earlier when I left Toronto for Nova Scotia.*

I don't feel like writing.

> Yet you are here, writing.

I feel like running, hiding, sleeping, burying myself from the world.

> Yet here you are here, writing. Celebrate that. Acknowledge it. Even if you did not write another word now, you have accomplished much. You have put fear in its place, which is in the background. You feel guilty about what you write, yes?

Yes. Am I using these dialogues as a crutch, just as I used journaling to avoid working on *The MoonQuest* in Nova Scotia?

> You were going to write something else.

I was going to say, "to avoid *real* writing."

> This *is* real writing. This writing teaches you to trust, teaches you to heed the call to write despite your fear. This is no crutch, not yet. Don't second-guess yourself. Trust your heart. Trust it and open it as you have never opened it before. Open it to others, yes. Open it first to yourself. That is your opportunity for your time remaining here in the north. You will be returning south to

Toronto soon, very soon, with a heart healed through openness, through vulnerability. For that is the only way to healing: through openness, through vulnerability, through risk. Through truth.

Be your truth. Live your truth. Speak your truth. Love your truth. Embrace your truth. Walk your truth. Walk it with confidence, with power, with empowerment. Whenever you feel it slipping from you, step forward and reclaim it. When you reclaim truth, you also reclaim love.

Love is coming?

It is here. Do you not see that you are already opening to what is present within and around you? You are like a bud, slowly unfurling its petals to the sun, petals that have been clenched together for too long. Feel the sun on your petals. Feel its warmth, its nurturing, its protection. Its love. Feel your own love, the love of your wisest self. Sit with that in silence for some moments.

All I feel right now is despair.

That, too, is part of the oneness. Don't deny any of your feelings, however ugly or fearful they seem. Acknowledge them all, then let go of the ones that no longer serve you.

Within seconds, self-deprecating, self-punishing inner talk accuses me of avoiding The MoonQuest.

Don't punish yourself. *The MoonQuest* will return as you and it are ready for each other. For now, trust and love yourself. Trust your truth, which speaks to you with such eloquence. And be. Be trust and you will be trusted. Be light and you will be enlightened. Be one and oneness will enfold, embrace and nurture you, will lead you to promised lands within and without. Be. Be the wisdom and divinity you are.

Thank you.

Namaste.

Tuesday, January 21, 1997
DAWN

As dawn breaks I set pen to paper in a free-flowing, free-writing, Muse Stream way. The result is "First Word," a poem whose final lines read, "First one word / Then another / And before dawn, the poem is done."

First Word
First one word
Then another
And another
And another
Unthinking
Mind-less
Heart-full
First one word
Then another
And before dawn, the poem is done.

Before dawn the poem is done. It's dawn. Is that a poem?

    Does it matter?

Strangely enough, it doesn't matter at all. What matters is that I woke up early, rose with relative ease and didn't run from the dark. I moved into and through the dark — my dark. I set words to paper — first one, then another, with little hesitation and loss of concentration, and now dawn's pale blue light has begun to spill in, mixing and melding with the flickering yellow of candlelight. Pale blue and yellow — the two primary colors that create the green of new life, rebirth, resurgence. I feel tired but good.

Your healing is wondrous to behold — both within yourself and through yourself to others. Your sense of oneness grows by the moment, for your oneness has always been present. There is still journeying to be done, but you know now you can travel in imperfection, healing yourself and others as you travel.

You worry about worrying about food. Let the first worry go, and the second will follow close on its heels. Draw yourself back to the now, gently and with love. Treat yourself with the same love and compassion as you treated the friends you inspired yesterday.

Yours is a life of service, to yourself as well as to the world. Serve in love and love will serve you. The more vulnerable you permit yourself to be, the more you open your heart to the world, the more you risk, the less you can lose. For there is nothing to lose, other than your expression of truth.

Thank you.

Thank you. Let your truth guide and protect you. Namaste.

Wednesday, January 22, 1997
DAWN

As I think about leaving Penetanguishene for Toronto, I recall a parallel moment — two years ago when I knew it was time to leave Nova Scotia. Now as then, I sense a need to not live alone when I return to the city. Now, unlike then, I feel called to seek out more than a solo housemate; I feel called to a communal living situation — my first ever.

I need to write. I don't know what I need to write, but I need to write through the stillness, through the fatigue, through the fear. And so, once more into the void.

    Congratulations.

For what?

> For trusting the blank page. For trusting the emptiness enough to enter into it on faith, the faith not of the ignorant but of the wise. For you are wise. You prove it every day to everyone you touch, even when you do not see it. Remember to see and experience within yourself what others see and experience of you. Remember to acknowledge it and celebrate it. Remember, too, that it is a great responsibility to live, as you do, from that place of trust, from that place of consciousness, from that place of wisdom and surrender. It is a great responsibility because nothing you say, think or do can fail to have an impact on others. Your love becomes everyone's love. Your empowerment becomes everyone's empowerment. Your fear becomes everyone's fear.
>
>   That does not mean for you to stop feeling what you feel. You must feel your feelings. All of them. For to deny any feeling is to create a blockage — within yourself and hence within the

> universe. So feel freely, fully, lavishly. Feel it all. The eagle cannot soar if his wings are weighted down with freight. Nor can he jettison that freight if he refuses to acknowledge its presence. So acknowledge your feelings of fear, doubt, distrust, anger and judgment. Acknowledge them, thank them, embrace them in farewell and let them go.
>
> Yes, these are words you have written here before. Write them again. And again and again and again until they are branded into your psyche, until they fuel every thought and action. You have fear now, yes?

Yes.

> What is it you fear?

I'm afraid of this new living situation I feel called to in Toronto: multiple housemates...a house full of people...everything out of control, out of *my* control.

> Control is not safety. Control is an illusion. Safety resides in your heart. Only in your heart.

I'm still afraid. Of the future. Of the past repeating itself into the future.

> See the dawn break through the dark outside. See it usher in a new day, dissolving the old one. The old day no longer exists, except in those cords that you have bound to it. Unloose the cords and float free from the old day, from the past. Float free and freely into the new dawn, into the new life that each new day represents.
>
> Trust your knowingness. Trust your calling. Trust your power. Do not deny it. Do your best not to fear it. When you cannot help but feel fear, see the word FEAR in your mind's eye and watch it dissolve and dissipate. See it be absorbed into the earth to be composted back into love. Let that love move you and move through you. Let it transform you and enlighten you. Let love be you. Let yourself be love.

Do you feel ready now to step into your day?

So-so.

> Then take your first step, however tiny and tentative. Let that step and all steps be steps of love and openheartedness. Let them be steps into the fullness of your soul.

I almost said, "I'll try." No more trying. I *will* it so. I will my heart to open. I will my fearlessness to triumph. I will myself into the void. I will myself into life and into the living of it. I choose to gratefully acknowledge and let go my fear of the unknown.

> Well-spoken. In speaking it you begin the process of freeing it to be so. Now, enter your day. Create it moment-to-moment, second-to-second. Create the present, and the future will take care of itself, will take care of you.

AFTERNOON

Here I am, hiding out in my bedroom. My whole system is in collapse.

> Nonsense. You are doing fine.

I don't feel fine.

> Much has happened in recent days and weeks. You need time to take it all in, to get used to the idea of living with a group of people. You have never done that before. Except for those ten months with Fred[1], you have always been on your own. Of course you feel anxious.

Those ten months with Fred weren't always easy.

---
[1] Fred was my first-ever roommate. I lived with him in Toronto just before moving to Penetanguishene.

> Perhaps not. But that was also a first for you, and you not only got through it, you graduated summa cum laude.

And now I'm going back to kindergarten.

> Hardly. You are going on to graduate school!

What happened to the empowerment of recent days, when I felt my fear and was able to disable it and flush it out? Now I feel helpless.

> This will pass, more quickly than it has in the past because you are stronger than you were in the past. Each time it will pass more quickly than the time before. Reclaim your strength. Reclaim your power.

I'm trying. I know I'm not supposed to say that—

> There is no "supposed to," just as there is no "trying." Just is. Be who you are, however unpleasant it may seem at times. Be your feelings, however ugly they may feel at times.

I want to eat.

> Using food to ease your anxiety is still an issue. It is much less of an issue than it was a month ago.

This feels like a setback, like a step backward.

> Look on it more as a pause.

Not one that refreshes.

> It is good you have kept your sense of humor.

I don't feel like this writing is taking me anywhere.

> Then stop. Return later, when you feel better able to surrender to it. Don't look for perfection. There is no right or wrong. There are no mistakes. There is only learning, growth, life and love. Be true to yourself and there is no failure.

At moments like these, I'm not sure I believe that.

> Then let it go. Feel your fear, but don't cling to it. Let it go and just be.

That's the hard part.

> But not impossible.

No, not impossible.

> Good. Breathe love back into yourself and light back into your day. Trust that all will be well. Trust yourself as others trust you. Be. Just be. Don't work at it. Don't struggle at it. Take it breath-by-breath. Stay as present as you are able to. If your mind wanders backward or forward in time, lead it ever so gently back to now, without judgment.

I'll try— You're going to say: "Don't try. Be." I *am*, then, and at this moment I am fearful.

> Perhaps in the next moment you will not be. Don't dwell on it. Know that you are doing fine, regardless of what you feel. You are doing fine *because* you feel. Trust that.

Thank you.

> Namaste.

EVENING

I've just finished typing this afternoon's dialogue. It's so self-pitying.

> Don't judge. That is where you were at that moment. Just because you are not there in this moment gives you no right to judge. In judging yourself you only harm yourself.

You're right. And it's not as though I have bounced back completely. I'm still feeling vulnerable, shaky, raw.

> That's okay. It is part of the journey. If you did not need to feel this, you would not. To repeat from earlier: Look at how far you have moved in such a short space of time. Stop to celebrate. Stop to praise. Stop to pat yourself on the back.

That would be nice. Instead, I stop to panic.

> Judgment again.

It comes so easily. Too easily.

> Be conscious of all you say and do, of all you think and feel. Be conscious so that you can recognize your patterns and shift them. Conscious awareness comes first. All else follows from that.

I came up with a new affirmation earlier: It wasn't about reclaiming my power but about letting universal power flow through me.

> The distinction is not important, unless it is important to you.

I don't want to get into an ego trip. You know: *my* power.

> You are in no imminent danger of any ego trip. Your self-image could still use a boost. If "my power" does that, there is nothing wrong with it. Use the words that work for you, but be conscious of the words you choose. For those words are part of creating or un-creating your reality.

I don't know that I have much else to say or ask. I just felt the need to check in after typing the previous dialogue. I have been writing a lot of these dialogues in recent days.

> And will continue to do so, for now. But you will reach a point, sooner than you think, when these dialogues will end, when you will be able to access and digest this wisdom — your wisdom — on the fly.

That will speed things up.

> Things are going to speed up for you. Fasten your seatbelt.

It's not going to be a bumpy night, is it?

> Only as bumpy as your resistance forces it to be.

I don't want to resist. Why do I resist so?

> Fear of change, of losing the status quo. You spoke of all that yesterday. Remember, again: All your words offered to others are first for yourself.

I know it. I speak it. Sometimes I forget it even as I speak it.

> Being a teacher and guide is first about teaching and guiding *yourself* into wisdom. You need your own wisdom as much as others do. That is why healing work is so healing: because the first person to be healed is you.

I don't know what else to say.

> There is nothing that needs saying, other than a reminder to open your heart, listen with your heart, speak from your heart and follow your heart. You once thought that the only way to survive was to padlock your heart and throw away the key. That may have been true then, for the feelings-numbed child you were. The enlightened adult you are now must know that the only key to survival is an open heart. Opened as wide as possible. Wider than you think possible. Be that open heart everywhere you go, with everyone you meet. That is how you will heal yourself and help others.

Scary stuff.

> Right stuff. Important stuff. The stuff of truth. The stuff of life. The stuff of love. Have you anything else to say or ask?

I don't think so.

Then stop for now. Know that despite today's fear, even because of today's fear, you continue to move forward with a relentless rapidity. Keep opening in each moment and yet more miracles will occur — so many miracles that all will seem like the single, never-ending miracle that is the truth of every moment, that is the truth of life.

Thank you.

Go now, in this infinite moment of infinite miracle. Namaste.

Thursday, January 23, 1997

MORNING

I see now that yesterday's crisis was about control, about me feeling that I need to control my environment — as if holding onto control would banish uncertainty and ensure my safety. An illusion, I know, but a very real-seeming one to parts of me. Thing is, if I had to surrender control living with one person, imagine how much control I will have to give up in a house full of people! No wonder I went into a panic. And it's no surprise that so much of my anxiety centered on the kitchen, given how much of my emotional survival I have invested in food.

Funny how control keeps finding new ways to show up in my life. They're not really new ways at all; they're more like deeper, more ingrained ways. All I have to do is remember the panic I felt three years ago [around moving out of the apartment I had lived in for more than a decade]. Well, this is another unknown, another level of uncertainty, another layer of control that needs lifting. There is no room for it or for the fear that its threatened removal engenders.

"So many miracles that all will seem like the single, never-ending miracle that is the truth of every moment, that is the truth of life." Did that come from *my* pen, through *my* heart? It's amazingly beautiful and apt. My challenge is to live that. And shared living on a larger scale is my opportunity to do it. I'm so fortunate, so grateful. Even in my clinging fear, I'm grateful. I feel so blessed. I have questions. I have doubts. I have uncertainties. But I'm blessed in them, through them, despite them.

What are your questions?

I was thinking about Pathlights when I wrote that I had questions. I just don't know what words to use to—

> To sell it?

I didn't want to write "sell." It feels crass and manipulative.

> Selling, for you right now, is about putting yourself out there, and not just to those you know to be sympathetic. It is about grounding yourself in your truth and speaking it come what may. It is about taking risks. It is about letting your thoughts, ideas and beliefs be heard and perhaps judged. It starts with selling yourself to *you*.

Suddenly, I'm thinking about food again.

> It is wise of you to notice the connection. Remember, no true harm can befall one who lives in truth, stands on truth, speaks truth. Living with people is an opportunity for you to experience that, to practice that, to be that. And you will.

Thank you.

> Namaste.

Friday, January 24, 1997

MORNING

Another open-mic at The Daily Perk. *Instead of reading from* The MoonQuest, *I share my poem "First Word" and a dialogues excerpt. I plan nothing else, other than to speak from my heart. What comes out are thoughts on writer's block and fear of uncertainty.*

Last night was amazing, phenomenal, wondrous, inspiring! I was ecstatic, on a real high.

> Acknowledge and celebrate your fearlessness, your openheartedness, your vulnerability. You touched those people last night, even if they did not consciously realize they were being touched. You touched them soul-to-soul, and that is where it counts. You are doing what you need to be doing, which is trusting, which is taking every opportunity to open your heart — wide, wider and wider still — and sharing it with others.

I'm feeling a bit of a backlash today — in response to that vulnerability?

> Yes, and fear of the future.

That feels right.

> Given the role fear has played in your life for so long, this is normal. Celebrate its weakening hold on you, even as you remember those places of fear in you so you can help others find those same places of fear within themselves.

I still have some trepidation about moving back to Toronto. I had this same feeling when I left Nova Scotia, when I knew I would be returning to certain friends who would wonder who I had become, who would question views and beliefs we no longer share.

Did you ever share them? Did you really?

On the surface, maybe.

> These friends have more respect for you than you credit them with. Even were that not true, their judgments could not harm you unless you were to give them that power over you. Don't hide your light under a bushel for fear of being rejected. Don't abdicate your power to others' judgment.

I have abdicated enough power in my forty-two years. I don't want to abdicate any more.

> And you have reclaimed much. Now it is time to continue claiming that which you have never wanted to exercise, out of fear; "continue" because you have already walked a great distance on that road. There remains much traveling to do, for it is a lifelong process.

Now what? I always seem to be asking that.

What do you choose?

I hate to use the word "utility," but in quoting from the dialogues last night, I discovered a utility in these writings that transcends my own healing. I find that very exciting.

> Don't denigrate your own healing needs. These dialogues must serve you first. Only through their service to you can they serve others. Others are not more important than you. That may not have been your intention in your choice of words, but that was the implication.
>
> Remember to be conscious of your words and thoughts, feelings and emotions. Remember that how you say what you say, how you express what you feel, the actual words and tone, speak more truth than your conscious intention. Your unconscious

mind always contains the seed of its own truth, and that seed will sprout — if not directly, then indirectly. That is why it is so important to listen from your heart, for only then will you know what is truly being said, by you or by another.

I'm fading. I think I need a nap. But I don't want to lose this dialogue.

This wisdom, *your* wisdom, will still be available when you awaken, for it is always present and always available. Go, then, and enter into the void of the dark, of sleep — and know that just as all is possible in dream, so all is possible in waking. For dream and waking are one. They inhabit different forms of the same infinity, of the same reality, of the same presence. You, too, are infinite, as is your wisdom, as is your vision, as is your power. They are boundless, stretching backward and forward in time to encompass all time. Go, now, into the infinite moment of darkness, the infinite moment of sleep. Return when the moment is right.

Saturday, January 25, 1997

PREDAWN

I need to write. That's why I'm huddled here on this dark, wintry morning, cocooned in a thick bathrobe and afghan comforter, a flickering candle my only light.

A plow scrapes by outside. One car then another slices through the snowy blue-gray light. The radiator clicks and creaks, trying to throw some heat my way. And the pen scrapes across this page, fulfilling some ancient, primeval imperative to communicate. Me to me. Soul to ego. Wisest self to not-quite-so-wise self. Unconscious mind to conscious mind. Dark to light. Messages. Many messages. Those traveling through my pen — heart to pen to hand to page — help still the other messages. Fearful messages. Malign messages. Nattering, chattering, carping messages. Woody Woodpecker rat-a-tat-tat messages.

Writing this way is a form of meditation. I never thought of that before, but it is. It's one of the few ways I can successfully sit in silence and let my inner life and inner voices carry me where they will. Some writing does that. Not all. Not yet. But I'm making progress.

I have finished my hot lemon drink so I can close my eyes — do close my eyes — and surrender yet more to the Muse that meets me here at this hour. Is it another poem she asks of me? Best not to plan. Best to let. To be. Or not to be? There is no question. The only answer is to be. Anything else is a betrayal of the gifts God has given me. Are you listening, God? Some days, some moments, I doubt that you are, wonder where you are. Some moments. Few moments. Far-between moments. I'm just rambling.

My first instinct is to judge myself for that. "Just" rambling, as if the mere act of freeing my pen onto the page weren't of value. Did I write "mere"? My eyes are closed so I can't read it. If I didn't write "mere," I thought it.

Judgment. Again. Still. I'm trying to still judgment. To be love. I see how important it is to watch my words. To be conscious. Vigilant. Aware.

I'm hungry. I feel emptiness gnawing at me. Am I rambling to avoid the emptiness? To fill the emptiness rather than letting it fill me? Don't fill it; feel it. The emptiness, that is. Am I judging, or am I running? This is feeling useless, as though I could just write these inanities forever and never accomplish anything through them.

> Judgment words. What about trust words? What about letting-go words? What about surrender words?

Surrender is dangerous. Surrender is messy.

> Surrender is life.

Not much to say to that. I'm struck speechless. I'm struck cold. Literally. My legs and butt are cold. Has the rad switched off? Dawn is breaking. I see the light filtered through my closed lids. Pale dawn. Snowy dawn. What happened to the wondrous, joyful dawn I affirmed when I woke up? What happened to the healing, restful sleep I affirmed when I went to bed? Perhaps it was healing; it sure wasn't restful.

> The sleep, the dreams, the wakefulness, even the restlessness: They are all part of the healing. When the rest*ful*ness part of the healing is needed, it will come too. For now, all you can do is surrender, all you can do is trust in the inherent wisdom of your experiences, even if that wisdom remains, in this moment, invisible.

We're back in dialogue. Did I really need that rambling preamble?

> Trust yourself. Trust your process. Trust your innermost needs. Let them play themselves out without question, without judgment, without fear.

I have a hard time distinguishing between, on one hand, feeling my fear then letting it go and, on the other, out-and-out denying it.

> That will come. As you experiment with new ways of being, there is bound to be some trial and error. Let go your nagging perfectionism, your nagging need to control. Acknowledge them. Say: "Yes, this is fear, this is control, this is perfectionism. Thank you for your stalwart service for so many years. I love you. Now it is time to let you go, to release you into Mother Earth. She opens her heart and arms to you. She will love you in my place."

She will kill me.

> She will transform you. There is no death. There is only trans-formation. Trans-*form*-ation. There is only change, the change without which life could not survive. Cells change. Seasons change. Leaves change. All must change or cease to exist. It is change that will keep you alive and strong. No-change will stop you cold. There can be no unchanging status quo within a present moment that rolls on into infinity.

Mercilessly, like a steamroller.

> Mercifully, filled with the love and compassion of the universe, which is infinite.

I'm not convinced.

> Are you more convinced than when you began?

Yes.

> That, too, is change.

I'm hungry and cold.

> You are free to go any time. This is not an endurance test. You have choice. You have free will. This is not punishment.

No, no, I know that. I don't want to run from the cold and hunger. I don't want to run from these words.

> Listen. Discern. Trust. All the answers you need are already within you. All you need resides in your heart, which is why it is so important to open it — wide, wider, wider still and yet wider still. Open your heart to yourself. Experience its richness.

Will I ever have a name for you, for whatever this is?

> There is no single name. There is no "I" or "we" or "us," for that would suggest a separateness that is not possible. What this is is universal consciousness. What this is is infinite possibility. It is all that is, was or ever will be. It is all the stars too numerous to count, even as it is the entire universe folded into a single atom. It lives inside you, so you could call it Mark. Yet it lives everywhere, so you could call it God. It is what holds the universe together, because it is the universe. It is that which cannot be named, because no single name could encompass the limitlessness of all that it is. Do you see how restricting and constricting a single name can be?
>
> The same is true for you, for everyone. "Mark" is a convenience. It can have no objective meaning when you are as limitless as this is, as all-mighty and all-powerful as this is, as all-loving, infinite and eternal as this is. For you and it are one.
>
> Remember your limitlessness. Experience and express your limitlessness. If love has no bounds, no one can steal it from you. If the universe has no bounds, there is no need or cause to cling to anything, for nothing is ever lost. Anything you let go of is always available to you and will be replaced in kind should that be necessary.
>
> Abundance is limitless; scarcity is a human construct. But like everything else, abundance exists only in your belief in it. Tinkerbell said to clap three times if you believe in fairies. It truly is that simple. Belief and its effects are that simple. Clap three times if you believe. And it will be so — not in the clapping

but in the believing. In the knowing. In the willing of it. Not as in willfulness but as in true will. As in willingness.

The movie *Free Willie* pops into mind.

A powerful metaphor for releasing what has been unnaturally caged and restricted. What is caged and restricted cannot express its limitlessness.

But limitlessness comes without structure, which means no control.

On the contrary. It means ultimate control. Moment-to-moment control. Not seeking-false-security control. The control of responsibility, not the control of shoulds and musts. The soft, yielding control of love, of trust, of faith. Not the hard control of mistrust, manipulation and fear. Therein lies the difference.

It's a big difference. I think I get it. I will do my best to apply it. Thank you.

Namaste.

Sunday, January 26, 1997

PREDAWN

I *want* to write this morning. Why am I so surprised? Because I want to write with nothing concrete to say? Yesterday I needed to write. This morning I want to write. And my "want" is softer, more yielding — more friendly — than my need. It just is. I want to set pen to paper, to communicate. To communicate what? I don't know yet. Maybe nothing. Perhaps gibberish. Will I judge? In this moment, I say not.

The silence was complete when I woke up. No snowplow this morning, no cars this early on a Sunday. Nothing but my breath, the dog's breath, the sounds of silence…that ringing in the ears that signals nothingness. Emptiness. The void. And I leapt into it, am leaping into it.

This silence won't last. It can't. Just as I will soon hear cars on the road outside, I will soon be moving out of my retreat and back into distraction, back among humanity, in closer and more intimate proximity than ever before in my adult life.

Even before I felt called to move into a house with other people, I sensed the arrival of more intimacy in my life. Of course, and not for the first (or last) time, this kind of living situation was not the means I expected or was praying for. As with all prayers, this one is being answered, but in ways that serve my highest good, whatever that looks like, even if I might consciously choose it to look otherwise.

Otherwise. Other-wise. That's where the wisdom lies. In the other-wise, in the unexpected, the unanticipated. In the silence. In the void. In the emptiness, which is where I am. Yet expectation still pokes its ugly head into the room. It asks: "When will these nothings turn into something?", not realizing that their very existence makes them something, not realizing that "something" arises not out of expectation but out of the unexpected, out of the void. Avoid. Don't avoid the void.

Images flash through my mind — of the park near my old house in Toronto. Why? A reminder of the Toronto that's to come? Will I be back in that neighborhood? Or is it meant as a reassuring view of the past as I sail into an uncertain future? Uncertainty. That's what waits for me. Uncertainty that offers strength and challenge and opportunity...and risk.

Risk. *Beau risque.* Is it worth the gamble? It's no gamble at all when you put your faith in God, which is only and ever your wisest self. That's what I'm doing here — what I have done all along, though sometimes in spite of myself.

I'm tired suddenly. Tired of, of...nothingness. Tired of emptiness. I want something, something to stamp these ramblings as worthwhile. I seek validation where none is needed. Where none is wanted. Where none is appropriate. Why did I feel better when I began writing than I do now?

> Because you move into the realm of the uncertain, into a realm you perceive as dangerous. Into a realm of fear.

Fear...again? Still? Always?

> Not always. But the precursor to big things, at least for now.

For now. For now. For news. News. Newspaper. Delivery. Carrier boy. Boy. Toy. Goy. Stranger. Strangers among us. Stranger in a strange land. Is that what I'll be in Toronto?

> No more than you were fourteen months ago, when you returned to Toronto from Nova Scotia.

Fourteen months. I have now been gone from Nova Scotia as long as I lived there, dwelt there. Dwelt. Funny word. Dwelling. In-dwelling. Out-dwelling. Outhouse. Out of the house. Waste. Taste. Haste. I'm impatient, impatient for something to happen on the page.

> What happened to not caring? What happened to being prepared to write gibberish?

I lied?

To whom?

To myself. I'm prepared to write gibberish if it leads somewhere, but not gibberish for the sake of gibberish.

> This is not gibberish for the sake of gibberish. It is gibberish for the sake of you, for the sake of freedom, for the sake of trust, for the sake of trusting the void.

Is that why I'm cold and hungry again? Fear of the void? Wanting to fill not feel?

> Could be.

Could be? Why no definitive answer?

> There are no definitive answers. All is uncertainty. All is change. All is flux. All is flexibility. Not like concrete. Concrete is definitive. It is certain, stiff, unchanging. Change is the force that places the greatest stress on concrete. Concrete cracks when too much stress is put on it. Concrete is weaker than air, weaker than willingness. You cannot stretch concrete. You cannot mold concrete once it sets. Concrete takes on form then holds that form. Concrete is inflexible. Concrete is no way to be.
> Flexible is the way to be. Flexible, open, ready to change, transform, grow, adapt, learn: these are the materials of the human spirit, the qualities that give the human spirit eternal life. For these qualities cannot be broken. These qualities stretch with growth, re-form with learning. These qualities are one with nature, one with natural life, one with—

For one is all, blah-blah-blah.

> Why the impatience?

It's the same spiel day after day. It never feels powerful as I write it.

> Silence your critic with love, not threats. It longs to protect you in the ways it always has, the only ways it knows how…or so it thinks. Reassure it. Tell it you love, cherish and appreciate it and that you need it still, but in new ways. Bless it, for without it you might not have survived to this day. Do all this, for it is part of you, and you harm all of yourself when you attack or inflict hurt on any part of yourself.

I'm sorry.

> Apologies are not necessary. Conscious being-ness is necessary. Love is necessary. Can you say what needs to be said?

I love all of me?

> Without the question mark?

I love all parts of me — all of me — unconditionally and without favor. I trust my inner truth, my inner wisdom, my divinity, to guide me, and I reassure those parts of me that are still afraid.

I tell them: "Trust me. I will not let you down. I will find new work if you still want to work. And if you choose to retire, I promise all the respect and gratitude that is your due for all the service you have performed on my behalf for so long. For without you, I could not be here today writing these words. You protected me. You kept me safe when I could not see my strength…when I could see my strength but not yet trust it; when I could not feel my own power… when I could feel my power but not yet exercise it.

"You have done your job with grace and honor. Now it is time to free me to do mine. Let me go. Let me let you let me go. We can continue together, but in new ways. Open to these new ways. I will protect you, if you need it, as you once protected me — until you can protect me in these new ways. We are friends not adversaries. Let us work together. Let us be the oneness we are."

> That was beautiful.

Thank you. It felt good to say.

> You may have to repeat it and if you do, don't be impatient, don't be unloving. Be love. That is all there is. All the billions, trillions and quadrillions of atoms and molecules in the universe — all they truly are is love, a love so immense and unchartable that it can only be experienced. It cannot be measured or mapped. It just is. As you are. As all is.

Are you finished?

> Still testy?

Parts of me are.

> That's okay. Give them a hug.

They shy away from my touch.

> Send waves of loving energy out to them. Let that energy embrace them, enfold them, reassure them. Much has changed. Much is changing. Much remains to be changed. It is hard for they who have known little change. But change they must, or die. Not the death of transformation, but the death of cease.

Not nothingness?

> No, because even in nothingness there is change. What will not cross the bridge with you will dissolve. It has happened before and will again. This is not a threat. It just is. What does not change cannot survive.

Nothing to say. Dawn. Silence.

> Time to think about winding this down and preparing for your day, another day of surrender. Are you still dissatisfied with these writings?

I'm more dissatisfied with myself for not be able to see their value as I write them.

> That is why it remains important for you, for now, to reexperience them by typing and reading them. Meantime, do not be hard on yourself. Do not punish yourself. Celebrate yourself. Celebrate yesterday's need and today's desire. Celebrate the fearlessness that has brought you to this place of creativity and revelation. Celebrate your courage and your love. Honor your fear, then let it go. Let go all that stands in your way. Acknowledge it and let it go. And trust. Trust above all — yourself, your divinity, your path.

Thank you.

I'm not up for five minutes when it's clear that the dialogue needs to continue, that I need it to continue...

I'm afraid. I realize now that I have been afraid all morning. I'm afraid of change, of the changes to come, of the changes that are already unfolding. I'm afraid of the brilliant yellow-orange sun that's just now rising over the bay. I'm afraid of that new light, of this new day. I'm afraid of myself. I have heard these words about change, about love, about release, day in and day out. Yet here I am — still afraid. And angry. Angry at myself for still being afraid. For not being man enough. For not being able to forge ahead.

For not being able to trample down your fears?

Well, yes.

> This is not about trampling anything. For anything you trample involves trampling parts of yourself, which is an expression of more than impatience. It is an expression of self-hatred. Love yourself. Love yourself as you love others. Feel toward yourself what you felt yesterday toward young Madeleine: an unconditional, protective, all-embracing love. You are still afraid? So what. You are human. You have much fear to let go. Don't dwell on that fear. Remember all the fear you have released, all the release that has brought you to this place.

But it feels like the same old fear.

It is not. If it were, you would never have left Toronto for Nova Scotia. You would never have left Nova Scotia to return to Toronto. You would never have left again for Penetanguishene. You would not be readying yourself now to leave Penetanguishene. Even if the root of your fear is the same, it cannot be the same fear, for you are not the same person. If anything, it is a deeper level of that root fear.

Celebrate all the courage that has brought you to this place, that has allowed you to touch this deeper fear. For only in touching it can you let it go. Touching it, not hating yourself for it. Touching it and loving yourself for it, loving yourself for all the trust, surrender and release that has brought you face-to-face with it today.

But I can't release it. I can't dissolve it.

You will, once you see it no longer has any real power over you. You are strong. You have the strength of hundreds. You have all the strength you need. The fear will vanish when you let it, when you release your grip on it. Only then can it release its grip on you.

Thank you. I feel better.

Good. Are you ready to face the sun? Are you ready to step into the day, to look toward the light, toward the uncertain, toward the unknown?

Readier.

Close enough. The day awaits, with all its challenges, opportunities, risks, gifts and treasures. Seize it and live it.

I will. Thank you.

Namaste.

Tuesday, January 28, 1997
EVENING

I'm exhausted. Is this genuine fatigue or emotional lethargy? Is it time for bed or am I yearning to escape the nothingness of another empty evening? Maybe it just feels safer to be unconscious in sleep than conscious in wakeful emptiness.

> Much that is big moves through you right now, at speeds you cannot begin to calculate. Fatigue is normal during such a time of explosive revolution. So are shock, mourning and grieving — even a kind of depression. Your fatigue and lethargy come from that same place. Don't run from it. Don't hide from it. Don't eat through it. Let it. In letting it, let yourself. You spent the day well, acting as you felt you needed to act, in the moment.

There were times today when I felt I should be doing more about finding a place to live in Toronto.

> This is not about doing. The time for doing comes. This is about being — being with the change, being in the change, being in the center of the storm of change. Let it all wash through you, like waves lapping at the shore, like surf crashing on the rocks.
>
> For now, there is no need to chase around for places to live. Plan to leave Penetanguishene during March, as you have intuited, and trust that the place you need — and that needs you — will find you when the time is right. That moment comes. In this moment, though, give yourself the time and space to digest and integrate all that is moving through you. As you do, do not underestimate the healing that has already occurred. So much healing occurs in the invisible. Open your eyes and heart to the invisible within you and celebrate it. Now, rest your heart, your

mind, your spirit. Rest your body for the journey ahead, a journey you travel already with such grace and courage, such fearlessness and ease.

Thank you. I will.

Wednesday, January 29, 1997
PREDAWN

I wake from a long, rambling dream during which I wander, disoriented and distressed, through my childhood neighborhood. My mood lightens when I bump into David Lieberman, a grade-school friend and an occasional dream visitor whose first and last names translate as "beloved" — David from the Hebrew, Lieberman from the German.

I feel tight with anxiety. I didn't linger in bed, but nor could I face the light. Everything I have done this morning has been by the softer, gentler medium of candlelight. Am I out of sorts because of the dream? It was an endless, convoluted stream of a dream that I chose to abort by opening my eyes. Was that an escape? Should I have seen it through?

No shoulds or musts. Just is.

I knew that as soon as I wrote it.

> Good and better still. The dream is but a tool. These writings are but a tool. What happens now happens deep within you: You find love. You find the *lieber Mann* within you. You find the wisest, most loved and loving self within you. No one way is better than another. Isn't that what you teach?

I know I journal most of my dreams, but I couldn't bring myself to spend an hour chasing after my memory of this one to the exclusion of everything else this morning.

> What you need to carry away from that dream lies within you, whether or not you are conscious of it. Trust that.

I'm afraid to trust.

> Nonsense. You do it now

To trust fully.

> Don't focus on what you feel you lack. Don't lose yourself in worry over the distance yet to travel. Celebrate the great distance you have already journeyed. You are here, now, writing, at this moment. However you got here, your pen skims along the page in total trust. Perhaps it will not be as trusting in the next. But in this moment you are willing and trusting. That alone is worthy of note, of acknowledgment.

I'm afraid. I'm cold and afraid.

> Of what?

I don't know. Of fear? Of life, new life? I'm afraid to let go…into the day, into the dawn. Emptiness looms ahead of me, stretches farther than my mind can see. It's like a huge swamp.

> Your mind needn't see its end. Your mind needn't see its beginning. Your mind need see only this moment. This word. This letter. This thought. This breath. This whisper. Let your mind rest in the present moment, in this stillness, in this now. The next moment will take care of itself — and of you — if you release into it.

I still feel somehow that I ought to be doing something about finding a new place to live.

> Ought equals should. When the need is to do, you will do. When the need is to be, you will be. Whatever the need is, you are adept at acting on it. Not with perfection. But this is not about perfection. It is about anti-perfection; it is about being comfortable in imperfection. It is about loosening your jaw, so clenched against the day. It is about loosening your body, so rigid against the day. It is about opening your heart, so closed against the day. It is

about acknowledging your fear without beating yourself up over it. It is about acknowledging it and, ever so gently, letting it go.

I'm suddenly so cold…so frightened. I want to run away, to hide, to escape from critical judgment…my judgment. I want to feel safe.

> You are safe. Look within. Look to the father you are to yourself. Look to the mother you are to yourself. Look to your heart — so big and open. Look to the divine wisdom that swells and grows within you as you unlock the gates that have held it back. There is where you will find your safety, the only safety that is real. Crave it not from the outside world. Seek it within and it will always be there for you.

I know all this and yet…

> And yet you need it repeated.

I feel so stupid. Like the student who just doesn't get it.

> Don't punish yourself. Don't judge yourself. You are doing fine. You are at the top of your class.

Then the rest of the class is stupider than I am.

> Nonsense and more nonsense. There is no stupid. There is no slow. There is no fast. Just is. You are where you are, and where you are is perfect — for you in this moment. You work too hard. Play some. What needs to work through you will work through you, regardless. Don't be so serious, so intense. Lighten up…into the light.

I'm impatient.

> Your impatience will propel you forward naturally. It speaks at this time to a certain readiness. Yet not to a complete readiness, for your fear speaks too. Love yourself and the fear will vanish. As the fear vanishes, as it does already, you will feel less need of the impatience. Don't worry at all. Be happy.

That sounds so trite.

> Clichés become clichés because of the kernel of truth that resides within them. You have it within you to be happy, to be worry-free. Of course you have that capacity. It is part of everyone, so it must be part of you, embedded in your emotional, spiritual and creative DNA. Like much else, it has been trained out of you. It can all be trained back. Not in an angry, punishing, repressive way. In a loving, inclusive, openhearted way.
>
> That retraining begins with you opening your heart to yourself. Such treasures reside there, treasures beyond your conscious imaginings. They are you, these treasures. Look within and reveal to yourself the wonder that you are, the love and beloved that you are, the *lieber Mann* that you are.
>
> Your heart links you to every other heart and their hearts to yours — when those hearts are open. To be clear, it is not the heart that is closed or fearful. It is fearful parts of you that lock the heart's door in place, that barricade it behind impenetrability. Dissolve those barricades and let your love and all love spread. You are safe in your heart. An open heart is the safest heart possible. It will cut through lies and deceptions, greeds and neurotic hungers — not cruelly and mercilessly, but like a knife slicing through soft butter. Wielded with love, it will encounter no resistance — neither within yourself nor others. Whatever ails you, whatever ails the world, the cure is always an open heart.

Why do I feel dissatisfied? I always want more from these dialogues.

> Your mind continues to rebel and resist. This shall pass.

I don't feel a whole lot better, and I don't know what to do about it.

> Do? Nothing. Be. Be in your unhappiness. Be in your grief. Be in your fear. Be in them. Let them be in you. And they will go of their own volition.

Some mornings, I have felt resolution as I approach the end of a dialogue. This morning I feel none, just continued anxiety.

> Then perhaps this dialogue is not yet complete.

I don't know what else to say, what else to ask.

> Then just be. Be in dawn's breaking light. Be in the cold of a wintry morning. Be in the candlelight. Be in the fear and anxiety. Don't run from it or try to erase it.

I don't want to feel this way. I want to feel empowered, excited, joyous.

> You create those for yourself — not by running or hiding, not by forcing or making it so. You create them by acknowledging, by trusting, by letting, by allowing. That does not mean a permanent state of false bliss. True bliss comes with the full range of emotions, including fear at times. It is about living — this moment, then the next and then the one after that. Don't use these writings to avoid living; use them to feel, to come out of hiding, to open your heart into the world. To share. To be vulnerable. To love.

Thank you. I think I'm ready to enter into the day.

> Then do it, in love and with an open heart. Namaste.

Thursday, January 30, 1997
PREDAWN

This dialogue follows another open-mic reading at The Daily Perk. For my presentation, I read "Into Infinity," a poem crafted from the dialogues, then I speak extemporaneously about the value of living in the present. When I finish, I feel inadequate, as though I have failed to reveal enough.

Into Infinity
surrender
to the boundless
All
that you are
immeasurable
unquantifiable
eternal
each moment a lifetime
repeating and unrepeatable
an Omnipresence that spirals inexorably
into infinity

I feel a pall of fatigue — of fear? — creeping toward me. I feel my left shoulder tightening up.

> You feel.

I do.

> Good. Now tell the feelings that you appreciate them, that you appreciate what they are telling you. Acknowledge them. Feel them. Breathe them in. Then breathe them out and let them go.

About last night…

> You did fine. You spoke true.

I'm not convinced.

> You showed great courage getting up there in total surrender, for that is what it was. That is what you did. The content was less important than how you presented it. Celebrate that rather than analyzing every word for its impact and effect. You intuited what you needed to say, what was needed for you to say. You spoke the truth your audience was ready to receive. This is not about bashing people on the head with your words but about leading them gently back to themselves, as you lead yourself back to you. It is about revealing, not forcing.

I didn't read out my bit about dreams and reality.

> Don't search for flaws. You will always find them if you do. Even if you had not touched a single soul in that room, you moved yourself. You moved yourself forward in trust, confidence and surrender. That is no small thing. That is enormous.

I needed to hear that. I couldn't quite trust it even as I think I knew it.

> That is why these words are here for you: to remind you of what you already know. That is why all teachers teach. That is the only true teaching, the only true guidance, the only true path-light. For what is teaching but shining a light on someone else's path, helping them see what is already there, what has been there all along.

What about today?

> What about it? Take it moment by moment, as you have been doing day by day. With each day it is easier for you to trust, to surrender, to be in and of the moment. It is that trust that is the source of your knowingness. Not blind trust, but logic-suspended

trust, which may seem "blind" to some but is never heart-blind.

Enter into your heart. Let others enter into your heart. Enter into the hearts of others. In doing all that, you will rediscover and experience yet more of the truth that once hid itself so completely within you. It hides no more. You have lifted the drawbridge, raised the portcullis and flung open the castle door to your heart. Traffic now flows more freely in and out of that soul-full place. Some barricades remain but these, too, dissolve with each day lived in courage and trust.

As you trust, so shall you live. As you open your heart, so shall you love and be loved. As you surrender, so shall your truth set you free — and help in the freeing of other barricaded souls.

Dawn breaks. Gray-blue light bleeds through my window and onto this page. It's time to meet the new day, to enter into it, to surrender into it heartfully, lovingly and fearlessly. I would like to say that the void holds no fear for me.

Then say it.

It's not entirely true.

Don't do "half-empty glass" on yourself. Your glass is more than half full. Notice that. Acknowledge that. Celebrate that.

You're right. The void holds — I want to say "little"… The void holds *no* fear for me. I dance with it willingly, lovingly, heartfully. I move to its song, learn from its silence, revel in its wisdom, live in its embrace.

Bravo!

That was hard, but only at first.

Hard *is* only at first. Cross that first threshold, that first portal, and all comes with more ease. Are you ready now to enter into the day, to surrender into the day?

I am.

Go, then, with confidence. And when it comes time to type your poem, don't judge! Don't criticize. Don't edit. Don't censor. Don't beat yourself up. Just enter into your poem as you enter into your day — with gratitude, compassion and respect.

Thank you.

Thank you, and Namaste.

LATE NIGHT

I return to The Daily Perk, not to be part of open-mic night but to listen to live music. I already feel anxious when I arrive, so I sit alone until some acquaintances invite me to join them. As the evening progresses, I grow increasingly uncomfortable "in the world" until, in the throes of what feels like an anxiety attack, I flee.

I was more panicked this evening than last night, when I knew I would be speaking. I tried to breathe out the fear and breathe in my power, but it wouldn't work for more than a few seconds at a time. Then my panic would return. What was that about? I don't like this feeling.

> Feelings are not to like or dislike. Feelings are. Just as you are. Don't run from them. If you do, they will always catch up with you. Of course, you still feel fear. There is too much history for it to vanish in an instant. Yet it is diminished: a spectral version of its formerly solid self. Celebrate that. Celebrate your strength when you feel your strength. Celebrate your power when you feel your power, even if it is only for a fraction of a breath. That is what living in the moment is about: staying present in your moments of strength, without worrying whether you can maintain them. Moment by moment. Strength by strength.

I still don't know what the panic was about…is about.

> Does it matter?

If I knew, maybe I could do something to reassure myself.

> You fear your power. You fear your strength. You fear your courage. You fear your beingness. You fear your oneness. You fear your connectedness, your interconnectedness.

There doesn't seem to be much I *don't* fear.

> Don't punish yourself. Just be. Be in your fear, and the fear will wash away on its own, sooner now than it would have at one time. Let your love for yourself wash over you, heal you, reassure you.

That's hard when I'm feeling as I'm feeling.

> That is when you need it most. It is like faith. You need faith most when it is tested, when it is stretched almost beyond its limits. You need love at those same times. Self-love.

I'm cold and hungry. I have wanted to stuff my face all evening.

> Yet you haven't. Bravo! Instead of denigrating yourself for your feelings and cravings, celebrate your strength in moving past them. Don't you see? You are stronger than your compulsions, than your addictions. You are strong. You are powerful. Yet strong and powerful does not mean feeling good all the time.

What does it mean?

> It means being conscious all the time — of your strengths as well as your weaknesses, of your steps forward as well as your missteps. Don't doubt your strength, even when you don't feel it of the moment. It is there, always. Choose to tap into it. You experienced earlier how your conscious breath could strengthen you, even if for a moment. Next time it will be for two moments,

then three, then four. Again, it is not about running from your feelings. It is about acknowledging them, then breathing them out.

Now what?

Let go the worries and obsessions of the day, the fears about tomorrow. Let it all go all and enter into the night with a clean slate. Don't plan out tomorrow. Instead, surrender to the present moment and tomorrow will take care of you when it becomes the present moment. For now, be conscious of your breath and go to bed, ready to meet whatever demons and angels await you this night. Whatever they are, they are there to help and guide you. So trust your experiences, your sensings, your feelings. Remember, there are no bad feelings or good feelings. There is only feeling. And feeling is good.

Thank you and good night.

Namaste.

Friday, January 31, 1997
EVENING

At four in the morning I wake to something. A dream? A voice in my head? My only waking memory is of a phrase that will become a mantra over the next days and weeks: "There is nothing so big that wishing can't make it so."

"There is nothing so big that wishing can't make it so." That phrase, that gift, has stayed with me all day. I have repeated it often, almost as though I can't believe it, as though I need to repeat it in order to believe it. It suggests — it does more than suggest — it insists that I have it in my power to create *anything*. That scares me. It speaks eloquently to the infinity of my power that so often comes through in these writings. I like to hear it, but it's clear now that it still frightens me, even if less now than when I first heard it early this morning. It must be less because I have gone from just repeating the phrase to actually wishing for things. I began by wishing for healing. "I wish to heal," I said aloud, then realized that I meant that I wished to heal not only myself but others too. Then, just now over dinner, I began to spell out what I wished to heal, in myself, at any rate: my limited vision, my repressed sexuality, an end to fear, just to name three on a list so long I don't now remember most of it. I know I didn't wish for ease, for an end to struggle. Why couldn't I wish for those? Never mind. I wish for them now. There is nothing so big that wishing can't make it so. It still feels big.

    It is. The biggest. Keep repeating it. Keep playing with it. Keep wishing.

I wish to believe that phrase with all my heart, with my full heart. I don't seem to have a whole lot to say beyond that.

Perhaps that is all that needs to be said. Not everything has to be grand drama.

Here's another first: I'm writing this on the computer instead of longhand. It's sure quicker!

> It is good to speed things up which are already speeding up! You begin to see that it does not matter how you receive these words. What matters is that your heart is open, for whenever your heart is open you will hear. Your heart will then move your hands, however you choose to write, until you no longer need to set words onto a page in order to access them, until you no longer need to move into a meditative space in order to access them, until you and your heart-words become one, regardless of where you are or what you are doing.

I'm tired.

> That is normal. Much moves through you at an ever-quickening pace. It is right to be tired, even exhausted sometimes. Remember what you told Lucy this afternoon and keep some of that for yourself: If you feel you need the rest, honor that. Remember, too, that you are powerful, that your power to change and to let change move through you is infinite, as is your power to fulfill your own wishes. Know that. Trust that.

My power to fulfill my own wishes is infinite.

> Open your heart to your wishes. Free yourself to wish them, to desire them and in doing so, you free yourself to let them happen.

Thank you. There is nothing so big that wishing can't make it so. Wishing can make it so.

> Wishing does make it so. Know that. Be it.

Thank you again.

> Namaste.

Saturday, February 1, 1997
MORNING

Funny sort of morning. Lots of mini-mood swings. From excited about the day to being unsure about it. From wanting to write to being uneasy about setting pen to page. And back again. Back and forth.

> Is this new, or are you now more aware of something that has occurred before?

Good point. The latter, probably.

> Increased awareness is always good.

I'm also noticing how often I have to redirect myself back to the now.

> Also good. Just don't swing yourself back with a sledgehammer. Swing back gently, lovingly, compassionately. Simply notice when you are moving out of the moment and let it go. It is the same for all outdated emotional responses and patterns of behavior. Acknowledge and let go, gently.

I've been thinking a lot about the move back to Toronto, and I'm finding that the line between excitement and anxiety is a thin one.

> Walk it consciously and with awareness, remembering not to let either emotion pull you away from the present moment.

"Nothing is so big that wishing it can't make it so." I don't know what brought that back to mind.

> Wish deeply and strongly. Wish lovingly and heartfully. But, again, don't let your wishes pull you from the present moment. This

> now, this single cell of a single thought: This is the present. Your present. Your gift. Life's gift to you. Neither hoard nor squander it. Be in it. Savor it. *This* now is your life. Not the next now, which cannot exist. Not tomorrow, which is illusion, which may never come. This moment. This word. This letter. This space between words, between thoughts, between breaths. So wish — profoundly, intensely, joyfully laughingly. But stay focused on the now.

I'm grateful for the reminders. I feel I'm doing better, but I wish to do even better, to remain present longer, more fully, less fearfully. I wish to surrender to the emptiness of each successive moment. I'd like to ask "what of today?" — but does that take me out of this moment?

> Planning is fine, as long as you don't lose yourself in those plans. Don't leap ahead in a fearful quest to fill a void, to end uncertainty. Yet don't use non-planning as an excuse for non-commitment and non-engagement. Stay as spontaneous and in-the-moment as you can. Find the balance.

As I sit in meditative silence, I hear this postscript.

> Let the fire of your divinity melt the glacier of fear that has blocked your path, and let the melting waters sweep through you, cleansing you of all toxins — physical and emotional.

May it be so. I wish it so.

> Then it will be so. It is so.

EVENING

I spend the afternoon on snowshoes, my first experience of the sport. What should be a pleasurable outing turns emotionally ugly. And the longer I trudge across the snowy field, the worse I feel — about myself.

I've been beating myself up. I'm not even sure why. I don't know that it matters. Right now, I'm filled with self-loathing — and fear, I now realize. I'm stupid and powerless and weak. Impotent. And worse — double all that — for feeling all this. I just want to die. It's not worth it. None of it is. I want to go on a rampage of destruction, self-destruction, and I might if I weren't such a coward.

I don't want to be reassured. I don't want to be helped or healed. I just want peace. I want this to be over. I don't want these feelings. I don't want anything — other than peace. To be left alone. To hide. To escape.

I want to trust. I want to cry. I don't want to die. But I don't want to live like this. I want my strength back. I want my power back. I want certainty. I'm afraid of this uncertainty, of this not knowing. I want to know. I want to understand. I want to feel my feet on the ground, to feel the ground beneath my feet. I want to be. I want to be right. I want to be well. I want to be healed. I don't want to feel these feelings. They're wrong. I should be punished. I am being punished — by weakness, by cowardice.

I want to move forward without fear. I hate this fear. I hate myself for this fear, this weakness. I want to love. Why can't I love? Why don't I love? Why don't I love myself? What has been taken from me that I can't love? Why has all this awfulness come about from ninety minutes on snowshoes? Please, please help me.

> Open your heart and feel the love that dwells there. Feel the love only you can feel. Feel it and don't hate yourself for anything you feel. Feel it and love yourself for having the courage to feel. Love yourself for your courage, for the courage it takes to come to this place of dialogue. Applaud your courage. Love your courage. Love yourself.

I can't. I don't know how.

> Of course you do. Love is as natural as breathing. It is the self-loathing that is unnatural. If God is love and God created you in His image, then you are love. It does not matter how you define

> God, what you believe of God or even if, in this moment, you believe in anything that carries the name "God." In the end, all God is is love because all there is is love. So if you believe in anything, believe in love.
>
> These feelings of inadequacy will pass, more quickly in your strength than you now believe. Yes, you are strong. You could not have journeyed this far were you not. That strength, your strength, all true strength, can only come from love. So the love is already present within you, waiting for you to acknowledge it. It is ready for you when you are ready for it.
>
> You have initiated your readiness by owning your feelings, by not running from them. That in itself takes strength and courage. Remember: Nothing is so big that wishing can't make it so. You wished for healing. This is part of that healing. It is a fire you must pass through in order to be transformed, in order to come out the other side reborn.

My mind understands every word. But I'm emotionally exhausted and still afraid. I just want to curl up and go to sleep. I just want to escape into the oblivion of the night. I can barely maintain my focus to continue here.

> Then sit quietly. Let yourself feel your strength, your power... your love. They are there for you to feel if you give yourself permission to feel them.

After a silent meditation, the dialogue continues.

> Parts of you are dying. Let them go. Thank them and let them go. They have served you well in the past, but they serve you no more. They are chains that slow your step. They are glaciers that block your path. Don't cling to them. Release them into new life so you can release yourself into new life as well. Trust the uncertainty, the emptiness, the void. Trust that great things will be birthed through that emptiness. Trust yourself and trust the divinity that surrounds you, that informs you, that co-creates with you, that is you. Trust the oneness of which you are an indivisible part

and which is an inseparable part of you. Trust, and be.

I'm scared.

> Of course you are. It is okay to be scared. Don't judge your fear. Feel it — in all its dimensions, in all its depth. Then feel the peace that follows. Feel the surrender. Feel the light that begins to move toward you through the darkness. It is your light, your divinity. Feel that. Be that. All else will follow and flow to you from that.

Even love?

> Love has never left you, never can leave you. It is as much a part of you as your skin, as your eyes, as your nose. Don't deny it. Be it — toward yourself as much as toward others. Toward yourself first, or you cannot be it toward others. Feel it. Feel it fully. Lavish it on yourself. Don't stint. Don't ration. Don't deny. Love is your right, your birthright. It must be, for it is everyone's.

Another meditative silence...

I feel better. Not great, but better. I'm still exhausted.

> You have surrendered to the dark, to the shadow. And in surrender, you have let go. Surrender is always a relief, a release, after so much holding on, so much clinging. Holding on is exhausting. It takes more effort to cling than to let go. To surrender is so much easier, so much lighter. Celebrate your surrender. Celebrate your release. Celebrate your wisest self. Celebrate your love.
>
> You are on the right track. You are on your path, true to your essence, true to your truth, even in the midst of your pain and anguish. Your faith is strong. That, too, is worthy of celebration. All of you is worthy of celebration. Believe that of yourself. Believe in yourself.

Thank you. Nothing is so big that wishing can't make it so. I wish to be healed. I wish to love.

> Then it will be so. It is so. Namaste.

Sunday, February 2, 1997

AFTERNOON

As I lie down, not sure whether to nap or meditate, these words of reassurance emerge in response to my anxiety.

> Whatever you spread in the world will come to you. If you spread magic, magic will come to you. If you spread healing, healing will come to you. If you spread love, love will come to you.
>
> Trust that you will be taken care of and you will be. Open your heart, and earth and heaven will open for you. Trust in love, in the power of love — in the power for love, in the power to love — and love will open for you, will open to you.
>
> Don't fret about *The MoonQuest*. It will happen as it needs to happen, when you are ready for it to happen. Let it go. Let all go but this breath, this speck of time which is all time. Surrender into it. Surrender and trust.

EVENING

I feel called to the page tonight.

> You feel called to your wisest self. That is good.

Life in community will be different from anything I experienced with Fred.

> A new experience. A new life. A new stage of growth. A new beginning. Your winter is nearly at an end.

I know, and I have been grateful for this winter of retreat. But I am ready to shed all this protective clothing winter has forced on me.

Shed those layers of protection. Your strength comes from within — from your faith, your love, your truth — not from layer upon layer of shielding, which is only ever illusion. Truth is the only garment you need. Wear it with honor, with pride, with love…for love. For you are love.

Monday, February 3, 1997
EVENING

This is a waste of time.

> There is no such thing as a waste of time. Time is infinite. You are infinite. Life is infinite. There is no waste. There is only growth.

Whatever. I'm afraid. Again. Still.

> Don't run from your pain. Don't run from your fear. Don't run from your loneliness. Know that every breath links you to every other breath, every word links you to every other word, every thought links you to every other thought, every life connects you to every other. There is no separation. There is no aloneness. All is connected.

More of the same. It's not helping. I'm still afraid. Panicked.

> What do you fear?

Change. Moving on. I'm afraid I'm not ready. I feel naked. I feel exposed. People will laugh. People will judge. People will destroy me, annihilate me. It's too much.

> You are in the midst of your awakening, your early spring. Your winter ends, as you have sensed. This is a season of coming out, of speaking out. Step out into the world and let the world see you — in all your eloquence, in all your wisdom, in all your power, in all your fear, in all your vulnerability. Walk the earth naked, clothed only in your truth. Not your certainty, but your truth. For your truth will free you, if you let it. Your truth will protect you, if you let it.

Fine words. They don't dull the pain.

> The pain moves through you. Yes, you are naked — increasingly so. That is good. Yes, you may be judged — when you begin to speak in ways you have never before dared. You will dare. You will have no choice. The words will demand to be spoken. In your courage and faith, you will obey.

In my folly, you mean.

> Not your folly. Your wisdom. You tap more deeply into that wisdom every day. You tap, too, more deeply into your fear — your fear of that wisdom. Feel your fear, for that is the only way to get to the other side of it.

I don't know how.

> Of course you do. You have done it before. You did it yesterday. You will do it again. Forgive yourself for your fear.

Hard to do from where I sit at this moment.

> "Nothing is so big that wishing can't make it so." Every wrenching letting-go, every jarring release — and all the pain that accompanies them — are part of the healing you wished for.

I don't like it.

> You have made yourself smile! So it can't be as bad as all that.

I'm as impatient as I am frightened.

> Impatience in this instance is good. It is a sign that you are moving. Just don't use your impatience as a whip with which to flog yourself. Be impatient and patient at the same time. Be compassionate. Be loving. Hug yourself. Father yourself. Be strong for yourself, even as you feel weak. This dis-ease shall pass, and you will emerge from it strengthened.

And in the meantime?

> Be in the moment as much as you can be. When you find yourself mired in back- or forward worry, nudge yourself gently and return, not in anger but in love and gratitude.

I don't feel any better.

> You will.

I know. But it's the present pain that is so hard to bear.

> It is the present pain you must surrender to. Only by surrendering to it can you strip it of its power, can you let it go...can it let go of you.

Once again, I'm totally dissatisfied with the course of this dialogue. Once again, I will no doubt recognize its healing power only as I type and read it. For the moment, though, I don't feel as though these words have given me anything I can use right now—

> To escape?

Touché.

> There is no escape. There is only immersion. From that immersion comes release. Which is not at all the same as escape.

I'm tired of this roller coaster.

> Then let go. Surrender. Don't cling. It is the holding on that causes pain. The letting go is freeing. Always.

It's that freedom I fear.

> Nonsense. You are stronger than that now. Stronger and more powerful. Know that. Believe that. Trust that. See how the power has manifested before and know that it will again, in ever more wondrous ways, as you tap deeper and deeper into its fullness.

Now what?

> Unclench your fingers, one by one, until your palm is open, until

your heart is open, until all that you clutched, falsely believing it would bring you safety, falls away. Feel the lightness now that all that weighted you down is gone. If you cannot yet feel it because you cannot fully release yet, imagine the lightness, the freedom…the floating, flying freedom. Without that weight you can soar with the eagles — so high that you see into both the future and past with ease. More important: You see the present in all its rolling infinity with perfect clarity. That is the gift of letting go. And you are letting go. It takes time and will to open fingers that are crabbed so tightly, but opening they are. They have opened so much—

Too much.

Never too much. They have opened so much that there is not much more opening left. Let them open. Let go expectations — of what this dialogue is meant to be, of what this moment was meant to be. Let go and let be, in the silence. Let go and know the divinity you are.

Tuesday, February 4, 1997
EVENING

On one hand, I'm eager to take concrete steps toward my return to Toronto. On the other, I'm anxious about leaving the perceived safety of my Georgian Bay retreat.

Why do I feel so wretched, so insignificant, so small?

> Let the fear pass through you. Don't stuff it with food and distraction. Feel the fear. Then let it go.

Oh, I feel it all right. I don't want to feel it. I'm tired of it.

> Surrender to it.

Are you crazy!?

> Ask it what it wants, what it needs. Don't punish it. Don't beat it up. You only end up punishing and beating up yourself. What is the fear about?

Toronto. Failure. The frightened parts of me are desperate for reassurance, for love.

> Whether in Toronto or not, you will feel success and you will feel failure, for that is the price of being human. Yet, in truth, neither success nor failure exists. No experience is that black-and-white. All experience resides between the extremes of black and white, in exquisite shades of gray, in vibrant rainbow colors, each melting into the next. Let the colors of your experience flow and float. Let them bleed into each other. Let yourself bleed.
>
> Feel all your feelings — the joy as much as the pain, the pain as

much as the joy. You cannot feel one without allowing yourself to feel the other. Feel the fullness of your feeling and you will feel the fullness of your being. Don't punish yourself for your feelings. Embrace them. Embrace them all.

It's so hard, when I'm feeling this way, to know when I'm punishing myself, when I'm indulging myself, when I'm not loving myself, when I'm disempowering myself, and when I'm listening and heeding.

Listen — to your body, to your heart, to your fear. Listen to all of you. Listen and discern. You will not always be right. But not being all right is all right. You are not perfect except in the imperfection of your humanity.

I'm afraid of leaving this cocoon of safety, of opening myself up in the wide world.

You want to say "in the bad world, in the dangerous world."

Yes.

Find that place in your heart where all is safe, where love is the only currency, the only food, the only water, the only air. Find that place. Live in that place, that place of love. And you will fear not.

Easy to say. You're not the part of me dealing with this shit.

You are smiling again.

Yes, at my childishness.

Smile at it. Laugh with it. But don't punish yourself.

I need to be free.

You are free. You have always been free. The gate to your prison has never been locked. Never. All it takes is a push, a tiny push. A tap. The tap of will. The tap of wish. One tap and the door swings open and you walk out into freedom. Do you dare tap that door, nudge it open? Do you dare walk out into the light, into the openness, into the unstructured, uncertain void?

I wish...

> Yes?

I wish to be healed. I wish to be free.

> Then live this discomfort, this fear. You are doing well, even as it does not feel that way, even as it feels as though the fear that claws at you is the same old fear—

It feels like I'm getting nowhere, like I keep getting bogged down by the same old fears, the same old shit.

> It is the same, yet different. It is deeper, closer to the core, to the root. You now touch depths you would never have been able to touch before. You do move, more rapidly than you know, more rapidly than you feel.

I don't want to be afraid.

> Then choose fearlessness.

As simple as that?

> Yes. Wishing can make it so. Start by saying it. You haven't in a while.

I choose fearlessness. That was easy enough. But I'm still afraid.

> As afraid as you were?

I choose fearlessness... Maybe not. There's a certain empowerment in writing those three words. It feels strong. They feel strong. I feel...stronger.

> You are stronger. Acknowledge that strength, that power to shift reality, to create your own world. You do not need to be afraid.

I feel like I'm getting mixed messages. On one hand, it's "feel your fear." On the other, "you don't need your fear." Which is it?

> Both. As you have written here before, you cannot jettison what you will not acknowledge. Feel it and let it go. However, if you begin by choosing fearlessness, you may not need to feel it, because it will not arise, because there will be no fear to feel.
>
> You don't need to be perfect. You cannot be perfect. It is not possible to be perfect. So celebrate all that you accomplish rather than punishing yourself for perceived lacks, for your fears. Celebrate, don't punish. Acknowledge your disappointment and let it go. Don't cling to it like a life vest. It is a millstone that will only drag you down. Now, sit in the stillness and find your inner wisdom and divinity. Find it, teach it and be it.

After a few moments...

I don't feel calmer.

> You are love.

Just like that?

> Just like that. You are love. Choose to be conscious of it. Choose to be aware of it. Choose to be love.

I choose to be conscious. I choose to be aware. I choose love. I choose to live in the moment, moment by precious moment. I choose life.

> Life exists only in the present moment, in this instant, in the breath between instants, in the silence between breaths. Breathe in the moment. Breathe in your courage, your strength, your will, your wishes, your truth. Breathe in your all. Do not fear your destiny. Embrace it. Embrace it with love and hope and gratitude.

I do. I embrace my truth. I embrace my destiny. I embrace all that I am. I write these words. I say them as I write them. I mean what I say. Yet the pall of fear doesn't lift.

It will. It has before. It will again. Wishing will make it so.

I wish to release all that holds me back, all that stands in my way, all that blocks my path. I wish to dissolve and eliminate all blocks and barriers, all constrictions and restrictions, all hindrances to the free and easy flow and expression of my divinity.

Well said.

Thank you.

Namaste.

Wednesday, February 5, 1997

MORNING

I wake up refreshed from a rare, dreamless sleep, ready to symbolically launch both my exodus from Penetanguishene and my "coming back out" into the world with a final presentation at The Daily Perk.

I'm thinking of going to open-mic night at The Perk tonight.

> Go and speak, from your heart. You will touch those you need to touch, those who will have come to be touched by you. The mere (and it is not at all "mere") act of standing up and speaking your truth — whatever it is, wherever you are — is always transformative, for everyone, including you. Don't rehearse your talk. Don't plan. Just be.

That's scary.

> It needn't be. Trust yourself, your wisest self. Trust your nakedness. Trust your readiness. Trust your truth. It will speak for you and through you, will give you the words you need, the words that those present need. See it as part of your contribution to *tikkun olam*[2]. *Tikkun olam* happens not through a miracle from above, but from thousands — millions — of miracles happening on earth. Miracles of connection, of interconnection, of heart-link.

I've lost the link to this dialogue.

> Don't let fear paralyze you. Don't let it deafen you. Don't let it suffocate you. Breathe. Breathe out the fear, the panic. Breathe

---

[2] *Tikkun olam* (pronounced tee-KOON oh-LAHM) is a Hebrew phrase meaning "healing of the world."

in your courage. Breathe in your strength. Breathe in your beingness. Close your eyes, breathe and reconnect with these words, with the essence of these words, which is the essence of you.

I still feel a bit shaky.

All is here for you. All is available to you. It is for you to seize it, to steep yourself in the love that is all there is. Every cell of your being is love. Every neuron, every atom, every hair, every follicle, every gland, every organ, every thought. It is all love. Be in that love. Be of that love. Be that love — toward yourself and toward others. Within yourself and outward, into the world.

Your call is to go out into the world with this love. Your call is step through all the walls you have built around yourself. You can step through them easily because the walls are an illusion. Walk through those walls of illusion. Let them dissolve in an instant. Blink them away. Enter into love, into the connected, interconnected, infinite and all-linked universe of love. Step into it, fearlessly, heartfully, clad only in your truth.

Your truth is all you have, all you need. It is all the protection you need, the only possession you need. You truth is your essence. It will set you free, and in setting you free it will help others find the freedom in their truth. That is your destiny. Be that destiny, the destiny you have been called to be. Take the next step into it tonight…and then continue the journey as you move into your exodus and beyond.

That was quite the pep talk.

You are ready: ready to hear it, ready to be it, ready to express it, ready to share it. It is time, your time.

Thank you.

Namaste.

With my winter's retreat nearly complete, a new life beckons — a new life in a promised land that is, itself, a portal to other promised lands. Each lies beyond the realm of my conscious imagining. Each is linked to the last by the spiraling road of another exodus.

Thursday, February 6, 1997

4:00 A.M.

I wake up from a dream about moving, in which I tell a woman who has come to help that she can pack up just about everything in the house because "I'm moving out after one more meal."

I would rather be sleeping, but I feel called to the page. Why?

> This is a powerful hour, this time before dawn, before the day is birthed. Commune with it. Enjoy it. Revel in it. Be in it.

It's hard when I'm so tired, so groggy.

> And thus so open.

No defenses, you mean.

> Fewer. Fewer with each passing day.

Part of me panics at that thought, but I know it's good.

> Defenses such as you are used to serve only to shut out the world, to shut you off from the world, to separate you not only from the world but from yourself, from your heart. Stay open.

I feel as though I'm in the middle of an exodus.

> You are. You are moving. You have begun to pack up to leave, as your dream suggests. You leave soon, sooner than you think. Many of your inner cupboards have already been stripped bare, emptied of patterns you no longer need, patterns that will not follow you to Toronto. So you move, faster than the speed of light — as the light you are to yourself and to the world. Just look at

the impact you have on friends, at how you help them open to the changes they grow through.

I put my pen down and within moments fall back asleep.

LATE AFTERNOON

I open my eyes from a nap and from another dream, only a single fragment of which follows me into conscious awareness: In the dream I have awakened at 12:12.

Twelve-twelve: a time of transformation, of new beginnings, of new awakening. A threshold time. I'm at a threshold, aren't I?

That you are.

It has left me feeling a bit unsettled.

Because?

I suddenly realize that these dialogues could be a book. It's not a new thought, but it's an idea that has always lived somewhere deep in the back of my mind. But now...

Now?

That dream...the feeling that I'm standing at a threshold of, of... something... Of "Dialogues with the Divine" as a book?

The song running through your head right now. Write it down.

"Good for the world in coming out / When we come out it's good for the world." This is not the "coming out" Holly Near sings about in her song, but it's just as big.

The thought of exposing myself with these dialogues, the thought of *really* doing it, brings up all sorts of fears. Again. Of being judged and ridiculed. Old issue, new expression. Is there a book in this?

> Would you like to see such a book?

No. Yes. I think so.

> Why?

I'm sure there's some ego involved. At a deeper level, there's a recognition that these words can make a difference to others, just as they are making a difference to me...that my experience is universal. Whatever I may fear about letting this material come out, I believe that. I trust that.

> Then you have a responsibility to see that you come out with these words in some way. But book or no book is not the issue. Coming out is the issue. Being out in the world with your truth is the issue. Trusting is the issue. Being your truth is the issue — not as a private pursuit, but as who and what you are, at all times in all ways.

That's kind of daunting.

> To your mind.

Yes.

> Your mind need do nothing, other than trust, other than surrender to the greater truth within you. It is already doing that — admirably, amazingly. It will continue to do so. You know what you need to do, what your heart calls you to do, what you long to do.

To be me.

> Yes. Not part-time. Not in the illusory safety of your rural hideaway, but full-time, in every way, wherever you are. The world waits for you. Trust your words. Trust your message. Trust your truth.

Why am I so surprised that when I describe these dialogues to others, they accept it all at face value?

> Why do you think?

Because part of me doesn't?

> Part of you clings to your old, blinkered ways of being and seeing. Let go of the old. Surrender fully to the now, to the new. Surrender to your wisest self.

This is making me uncomfortable. Part of me wants to wrap this up and run.

> Yet you don't. See how brave you are? See how committed you are?

I keep saying that I want to heal.

> Precisely. This new coming out is part of that. Like all forms of coming out, it is part of your responsibility to the world. It is "good for the world," as the song says. It is also part of your responsibility to yourself.

Again, *is* there a book in this?

> Again, do you want there to be?

I think so. Yes.

> That is more definite than just a few minutes ago. If you desire it, then wish it, will it, see it. And it will be true — in the way that best serves you and it, in the time that best serves you and it. Nothing is so big—

That wishing can't make it so. I wish to not be so afraid. I wish to be fearless.

> Then choose it. Choose fearlessness.

My pen hovers over the page, but I write nothing.

You hesitate.

Damn right! Part of me holds me back. But I'm stronger than that, more fearless than that. I choose fearlessness.

Whatever the cost and consequence?

Whatever the cost and consequence. There is no other way to be. Yet I'm still afraid.

The fear will pass.

What do I do now?

Nothing. Know your desires. See your desires, and move toward them. Embody them. You want this to be a book? Then let it be a book. Let it be whatever *it* needs to be. Don't prejudge. Don't force. Don't push. Let. And all will be as it needs to be, as you need it to be. Wonders await you. Recognition awaits you. Love awaits you.

Destruction awaits me.

Only if you will it so.

Touché. I create my own reality. So I choose a reality grounded in love, courage and openheartedness.

Good. You will be fine. You are fine. So stand up and stand out. Be yourself in the crowd. The crowd will only honor you for it.

Truly?

Truly. At a soul level for sure. At an embodied level far more than you fear. You are safe. Life is safe when you believe in yourself, when you live your truth.

I feel better. Still a bit shaky and afraid, but better.

Go now and be. Be in your truth. Trust your truth. Broadcast your truth. For your truth is the fire that burns away the old, that ignites the new. That fire is you. Express it. Share it. That is your mission. That is your quest. That is your calling. That is your destiny.

That is my choice. Thank you.

Namaste.

Friday, February 7, 1997

EVENING

In a repeat of my Daily Perk anxiety attack[1], I take myself to a local production of the musical Nunsense *but flee the theater at intermission.*

I'm embarrassed and ashamed. I feel so stupid and weak. I couldn't stay. I just couldn't. I could barely breathe.

> Don't beat yourself up. You were anxious. You left. Why is that a problem?

I feel like a ninny.

> You recognized your anxiety. That is good.

It doesn't feel good enough.

> Would anything be good enough…short of perfection?

I don't know. I keep wishing for fearlessness. I didn't feel very fearless at the theater. I don't feel very fearless now.

> You act despite your fear. That is courage.

What was courageous about what happened tonight?

> You were courageous this afternoon. You launched your exodus: You picked up a copy of *Now*[2] and scanned the ads for communal living situations in Toronto. You did more than that; you made phone calls. That is big. Acknowledge that. Celebrate that.

I do. It's just hard to celebrate when I have this backlash afterward.

---
1 See January 30 (late night) entry.
2 *Now* is Toronto's weekly alternative newspaper.

> What you move into is new for you, big for you. Give yourself permission to feel your anxiety, to feel it and let it go.

I want to let it go. I just don't want to feel it.

> You must feel all you feel. Only by feeling can you be free.

I ran from the theater like a weasel, like a rat…like the coward I am.

> *Nunsense* was unimportant. If it could not free your mind from your anxiety, if it made you feel more anxious, then it was not the best place for you to be tonight. It was okay to return to the safety of your home to work through your feelings.

I thought safety was only inside.

> You confuse the issues.

What are the issues? I am confused. Frightened and confused. I feel disconnected. I want to feel connected. I want to feel love. I want to feel.

> You do feel. That is what causes your anxiety. You feel. You feel deeply. Feel the feelings and move on.

It's all about moving on, back to Toronto, into a rebirth, into the community/communal/co-op that will challenge my ways of living, my ways of being. It's exciting— I can't believe I wrote that. That isn't what I meant to write.

> It is, or you would not have written it.

I suppose.

> And it is exciting, isn't it?

And scary.

> Both can exist side-by-side. One need not exclude the other. Be excited, and be as scared as you need to be so you can let that fear go. Celebrate what you achieved instead of beating yourself up

for your fear. You are a caterpillar breaking through your cocoon right now. That is not an easy task, but you do it. Break through that cocoon. Break free. And fly.

Thank you. I will fly. I choose to fly. I choose flight. Not the fleeing kind of flight, but the freeing kind of flight. I choose to be fearless. I choose to believe. I choose to trust. I choose surrender. I choose love.

Good choices all. Namaste.

Saturday, February 8, 1997
4:00 A.M.

It's funny: I woke up feeling fine (going to bed with "I choose fearlessness" on my lips probably helped). It was only when I remembered last night's anxiety attack that my mood and energy threatened to shift. I caught myself, and I seem to be okay now, even as I'm still nervous about Toronto, about finding the right place, about a co-op/communal lifestyle.

> But you have no doubts, no second thoughts?

None that is serious. None that gets in my way. That doesn't stop me from worrying some.

> You worry much less than before. You will worry much less in the future. Keep returning to the present moment, to the present sensation. Be aware of your body. Feel your feet on the ground. Feel your breath, the power of your breath, the wisdom of your breath. Feel the pen in your hand skimming across the page, swimming across the page.

Not drowning, as once I might have said.

> No, you would not have, although you might have felt that way.

I wonder if the woman next to me at the theater last night picked up on my anxious energy.

> You project what you feel. It is always picked up, even if unconsciously.

In the end, I was alone — an empty seat on either side of me.

You had disconnected from life, so life disconnected from you. But it didn't last. And here you are.

Here I am. Ready, I think, to go back to sleep.

Sleep, then awake refreshed, fearless and alive.

Thank you.

DAWN

I choose fearlessness. I enter into this day empowered, filled with joy, courage and humility. I enter into this new dawn and into each moment of this new day imbued with the spirit of grace, alive with the spirit of truth, true to my oneness in all its beauty, in all its splendor, in all its exultation. I open my heart to the world. I share my heart with the world. I live my truth. I speak my truth. I am my truth.

Well spoken. Embody those, and you embody life.

I choose to. I choose to be. I believe I can. I know I can.

Then it will be so, for it is already so. Namaste.

EVENING

When I first feel called to leave Toronto, it is not Penetanguishene that draws me to it but Lefroy, another rural town north of the city. I have a synchronistic reunion there with a childhood friend, I find a waterfront flat I love, and for two weeks everything about the place feels perfect... until the apartment falls through and I let Lefroy go. Now, another promising living situation — a cooperative household on Toronto's Ossington Avenue, has also fallen through.

I know there's no reason to feel disappointed. I know it must be for the best. So why am I so upset that the house on Ossington didn't work out?

> You know the answer.

Because I wanted a quick fix, an instant solution, an end to the uncertainty?

> And now you must wait for the right place — in patience, in trust, in uncertainty.

Just as I had to wait after Lefroy fell through.

> No, not just as. Then, you waited in anxiety. Now you can choose to wait in calm, in trust, in surrender.

I want to. Why am I anxious?

> Because you want that quick fix, that instant solution, that end to your uncertainty. Focus on the journey, not the destination. Remember that a process *is* a process. Once started, it can take time to complete and, as such, requires from you patience and, of course, trust.

I suppose it's no accident that I spoke to Odette about trust and patience this afternoon.

> You know there are no accidents, right? Just as there are no coincidences?

Of course.

> You are smiling. You smile more and more during these dialogues. This is good.

It feels good to smile, to smile at myself, with myself. To smile at my foibles, at my weaknesses, to smile through them and past them. I will be all right.

> You already are. You do what you need doing and, as you reminded Odette about her own journey, you are on the right track. All is unfolding perfectly. Your perfect place will find you.

I do trust that.

> Not fully.

No, not fully, or I wouldn't be carrying this residue of anxiety.

> A smaller residue than after Lefroy. It will pass much more quickly than it did after Lefroy and you will soon find yourself back in trust, back in surrender, back in your heart.

That is my place: in my heart. That's where I need to be.

> You are there, mostly.

I know if I ask, "What do I do now?", what will come out of my pen will be something like "Don't do, be" or "You're doing all you need to be doing. Trust that. Trust your process. Trust yourself."

> That's right. Soon you will not need to write in order to access these words of wisdom, *your* wisdom. You will access them on the fly, as it were. You move in that direction already.

I'm writing by candlelight, as I do so often after dark. Nearsighted though I am, I am also writing without my glasses. I lean into the page a little too closely...and burn the tip of my nose!

I can't believe I was so stupid as to burn my nose.

> It was a reminder for you to feel your nose, to feel with your nose, to trust your intuition. By trusting your intuition, you will find your new home. Rather, your new home will find you.
>
> Still, this is not about waiting passively. Even in trust, there is action required from you. Even in surrender there are steps that

you are called to take. You must pick up the newspaper and look through the ads. You must intuit which ads sound right, make the necessary phone calls and discern which merit a next step and which do not.

You have begun to do all that. You are trusting the reality you are creating. Continue trusting — until the very last moment, if that is what you are called to do. You will not be abandoned. You will not be homeless. You will be provided for. Your new home, your new community, is waiting for you to let it into your life. Trust that.

I do. I'm ready.

Then it will be so. Then it will come.

Thank you.

Namaste.

Sunday, February 9, 1997

EVENING

This has not been an easy day. It has had its lighter moments, but it started out difficult and has largely remained so...which is why I am already in bed, still trying to digest my lunch of nine hours ago. I have been hard on myself today. I have been punishing. I have not been conscious where food is concerned. Why do I slip? How do I slip? I don't want to slip. I don't like it, or me, when I slip. I don't like it, or me, when I punish myself, or try desperately to make perfect what's wrong by trying to force a fix on it.

> Stop trying to be perfect. Stop responding in fear and panic. Stop punishing yourself when you do respond in fear and panic. Give yourself permission to be imperfect. Be in your light but be also in your dark. Be all of you.

I'm tired. I don't want to be here, doing this. I want to put down my pen and try to sleep, even though it's only nine o'clock.

> *Try* to sleep. *Try* to *make* perfect. Are you conscious of your words? Don't try. *Be.* Don't make. *Let.* Don't force. *Relax.*

This has not been a good day for relaxing.

> Things are happening. Things are working through you, being pushed out of you, being jarred free. Respect the process and respect yourself. Love yourself. Let happen what needs to happen. Surrender. Surrender control. Control is a toxin, an emotional toxin, a toxin of fear. Let it go. Let it go and surrender to your wisdom. The wisdom of the ages lies within you. It is only for you to sit back and let it bubble up into consciousness to fill the emptiness you create through your surrender. Let it

happen. Let yourself happen. Emerge. Emerge from the cocoon you have woven around yourself and fly free into the world, into the uncertainty. Into the void.

I'm having a hard time even surrendering to this process, which I have surrendered to so often in the past. I worry about being able to decipher this scrawl, about having get out of bed to type it up while I can still read it.

Does any of that matter?

No, I suppose not.

There are no obligations, no shoulds, no musts. This wisdom is always part of you. It is not going anywhere. If you miss typing it this time, there will be other times. Let go that bit of control. Let go your obsessiveness. Let it all go. Let go and let be.

I need to stop. I need to sleep.

Then put down your pen and sleep, and let the night enfold you in compassion and forgiveness, toward yourself.

Thank you.

Namaste.

Monday, February 10, 1997

AFTERNOON

I spend the morning journaling the night's many dreams. In one, my mother suggests that I join a new spiritual group she has heard about. "I don't want to be locked into someone else's creation," I respond in tears. "I need to create something of my own."

> You do create something of your own. You do find your own way. You do blaze your own path. When you live from a place of trust in your innermost wisdom, you cannot help but create something unique. You do that now with these words. You will continue to do that with *The MoonQuest* and other writing, when the time is right. You will do that with Pathlights, however that comes together.
>
> You have traveled a long journey to reach this place. You have surrendered so much control, freed yourself in so many ways. You are lighter now — even as you are weightier. You are more substantial — even as you are a feather, the feather of an angel wing that floats on the gentle winds of surrender.

That's beautiful.

> These are your words, no one else's. This is your creation, your truth finding form and shape in words. As it does, it finds form and shape in your conscious mind.

Which is not rebelling as once it did.

> That is the beauty of surrender.

I still have difficulty stilling the inner chatter, surrendering to the void.

> Don't try. Let the chatter chatter. It will chatter itself out when you cease to accord it any power. Let it be, and it will wind down of its own accord. You are getting there.

It feels as though I have a long way to go on that one.

> Not nearly so long as you think.

I'm proud of these writings, even as I'm humbled by them.

> Not a bad combination.

I want to ask where they take me, but I don't want to be materialistic about it.

> You know the answer: They carry you into your own healing. They carry you into the healing of others. They can be a book, if that is your choice…if that is the choice of these writings, which, as you will discover, have a will and imperative of their own. For now, keep following your pen — not worrying, not judging, not censoring — trusting in the moment and in the word of the moment, in the now. Do that and whatever needs to happen in your life and in the life of these writings will happen, naturally.

My mind does wander at times.

> But you no long judge yourself for it. You have grown skilled in bringing yourself back to the now, to the pen skimming across the page, word by word.

You're right. I never saw just how clearly my writing had become a metaphor for staying in the moment in the rest of my life.

> That is why the fact of these writings has such power for you. Even through your doubt, you persevere. Even when you find yourself censoring or judging or drifting, you catch yourself and return, gently, to the path of wisdom, the path of trust, the path of surrender.

I never saw it before.

> Now that you see it, you can broaden its application. You can let it work for you in other parts of your life. You can begin to release your need to use pen and paper to stay focused on the present moment, on the eternal now.

How, now, brown cow. I'm being flip. I'm sorry.

> Not at all. "How, now, brown cow" is an inquiry into the present moment, into this instant. It is "How, *now*." And now is all that matters, all that counts. So, you see? Don't censor what you perceive as silliness. It contains more truth than you consciously know. Always.

A good reminder of my own words from when I teach writing.

> Those words will always serve you well. They are your wisdom, a wisdom that is broader and deeper than you now recognize, than you credit yourself with possessing, a wisdom that is always present and available to you. Always and in all ways.

Thank you. Thank you for the reminders.

> Namaste.

Tuesday, February 11, 1997
DAWN

It is not uncommon for me to hear a sentence or song fragments as I drift awake. This morning I hear, "Basically, we're wrong. One of the wrongest things in our lifetime is to—" I pick up my pen to find out just what that "wrongest thing" is.

Is to what?

> Is to live in your head. Is to vacate your body and dwell only in your mind. Such a lifestyle is unbalanced and leaves no place for spirit, no place for heart, no place for wisdom, no place for love. Your mind wants to be in charge. It cannot if you are to experience and express life, love and wisdom at their fullest potential. Don't abandon your mind. It is a powerful and necessary tool. But don't let it take charge of the journey, for its vision is limited. Only your heart-vision is infinite. Lovingly ask your mind to release its grip on your heart...on your life. Start by unclenching your fist, which grips the pen so tightly in this moment. In unclenching your fist, you will also begin to unclench your mind.

I see a bird in the palm of my hand now that I have unclenched my fist — a tiny bird, its delicate wings fluttering. I feel its tiny heart beat with explosive power and force. Now it grows *Alice in Wonderland*-like from tiny to gigantesque, from hummingbird to eagle. Yet it still somehow perches on my hand. It gazes at me with golden eyes, with a look of both challenge and love. It dares me to fly with it, not on its wings but on my own. In that moment I sprout wings — giant white feathers, ribbed in strength and power.

I'm reluctant, but I'm flying. I'm afraid, but I'm flying. Part of me tries to drag the rest of me down, to suspend this miraculous flight. But I want to fly. I choose to fly. Now, that fearful part of me has won. I'm not flying anymore. I'm weighted down, back on the ground. Alone.

> Let go. Let go the past. Let go all that encumbers you, all that weighs you down, all that holds you back. Unclench. Unclench your jaw. Unclench your shoulders. Unclench your body. Unclench your mind. Unclench your heart. Believe. Believe in possibility. Believe in miracle. Believe in yourself.

I want to. But part of me just stands there, immobilized, unable to leap back into the air.

> Breathe. Breathe out the fear. Breathe in the power, the power to soar, to glide, to fly, to be free. To see. The power of your vision. The power of your spirit. The power of your soul.

It is taking a tremendous act of will for me to get up and going this morning. Is that why my bird-self is grounded?

> Don't push. Don't force. Know that you possess the power, and that that power will manifest for you when you are ready. In broad terms you are, of course, ready. But each day is different. Each moment is different. If you feel unable to fly in this moment, don't punish yourself. Just be. Be all you are in this moment. Feel all you are in this moment.

I feel tired, hungry, somewhat stuffed up. Dry lips. Gas. Tight-assed. Always tight-assed.

> Loosen up. You do loosen up. Ask why the tightness at this moment. Ask why the fear at this moment.

Change. It feels as though change is moving through me at such a rapid pace — so rapid I can't see it. It's all a blur. I don't know what's happening, what's changing. I only know that something is. And I'm impatient, impatient with these words that keep repeating, yet nothing seems to change...even as it feels like everything is changing. It's confusing. It's scary. I feel like crap, like shit, like a failure. I want to die.

> You do die. You die out of the past to be reborn into the present. Let the death and rebirth happen. Give them the time they need. Allow your rebirth the pain, like childbirth, it may take. Know that with this change, this new birth, you lose nothing and gain everything.

I know all this. Why can't I feel it?

> You have before. You will again. For the moment feel what it is you feel. Feel the panic. Feel the fear, even the self-loathing. Don't cling to them. Grant them their freedom and they will grant you yours.

This is going nowhere. We're just going in circles. Again.

> All is a circle, a never-ending journey of oneness. A circle like the O in the word "oneness." More than a circle, it is a spiral. You spiral forward. You are not stationary. There is movement. There is always movement.

I'm losing my focus, if I ever had any this morning.

> Breathe. Breathe yourself back into focus, back into your heart, back into love. Breathe back into the eagle, into the mighty eagle you are. Let that bird have its freedom; the hummingbird too, for they are both you. Breathe out your fear. Breathe in your courage. Then breathe in your fearlessness. Choose fearlessness. Choose it now.

I choose fearlessness. I say it. I don't know that I believe it, that I can do it.

> Saying is a step toward letting.

I choose fearlessness. I choose strength. I choose empowerment. I choose to enter this day filled with the light of the new dawn, the light of love, the light of trust. The light of surrender. The light of healing.

> Well said. Nothing is so big that wishing can't make it so.

I wish it. I still feel shaky and vulnerable.

> Vulnerable is good. No one asks for invulnerability.

I do. It feels safer.

> Your vulnerability is a gift, and not only to you. What was on the card you received in the mail yesterday from Trish?

"Thanks for encouraging my soul to sing."

> How did it make you feel?

Touched. Honored. Gratified.

> Deserving?

Maybe. Not safer.

> The safety you seek by armoring yourself in invulnerability is illusion. True safety lies only in vulnerability, in an open heart — open to yourself and open to others.

I started to write "invulnerability" back there, even as I heard "vulnerability."

> It is good for you to acknowledge that which, in the past, you would have censored. There is good to be found in every experience if you are open to seeing it. Always. There is never a need to punish. To correct, gently, but never to punish.
>
> For now, leave the perceived safety of your bed and enter into the dawning light of a new day. Trust the day that awaits you. Trust your vulnerability. Trust yourself. Get ready to fly.

Thank you.

> Namaste.

Wednesday, February 12, 1997
EVENING

I'm afraid, afraid of the dark, afraid to sit in the darkness alone, afraid to sit in the darkness without pen in hand, afraid of what might emerge, afraid that nothing will emerge.

> Trust. Trust the dark. Trust yourself. Trust your divinity. Trust your self, your wisest self. Trust all. Set down your pen and trust.

Thursday, February 13, 1997

MORNING

I wake up with these lines from singer/songwriter Eileen McGann's "I See My Journey" playing in my head: "I close my eyes and pray for guidance on the road / For peace and joy and strength to bear up any load."

A good wake-up line. I need guidance this morning. I'm still haunted by Trish's question last night: "Do you see yourself as a spiritual prisoner or as a warrior of the spirit?" I don't want to see myself as a prisoner of any sort — or as a warrior, for that matter. It goes against everything I believe in, everything I teach. And yet...

And yet?

Perhaps I am a prisoner. I feel as though I am returning to a too-familiar place on my spiral of learning: a place of joy-denying asceticism that takes everything too seriously, that sees even fun as needing a concrete purpose. Even when I seem to opt for fun — snowshoeing, *Nunsense* — the pleasure is drained from what quickly becomes a serious exercise in painful learning. If that's not prisoner-like, it's certainly monastic. That can't be right. I write about life as a joy-filled, creative enterprise. Why do I fail to see that, fail to live that? Why am I caught up in self-denial? Why do I, like a Midas in reverse, turn gossamer into lead? Why do I even use words like "enterprise"?

> First, know that all is not as dire as you paint it. Know, too, that in recognizing the imbalance, you leap a great distance on the road toward a healthier balance. Life is play, and the play of life need not be grand drama or painful melodrama. Yes, pain is part of life, but so is play, laughter and joy. Play forms the bedrock of

creativity, so it must also form the bedrock of life, for life and creativity are one.

You are right to raise this now, to seek answers now. But, in truth, there is nothing to seek. Joy is innate within you. There is no need to reach in and dig for it. As with everything else these words address, it is about surrender. Let go and the joy will surface of its own volition. Let go and bubbles of laughter will rise — lighter than air — through your being and emerge from the night coated in rainbow colors, like soap bubbles, with every word you speak. Let go and play will become natural, will seem the natural activity it is.

You already walk a joyful path. Roxy has contributed to this. Jeremy has contributed to this. Your own questionings and actions have contributed to this. Now is the time for awareness. Now is the time for conscious choices. Now is the time to chose joy as you have chosen fearlessness. Choose joy. Choose it now.

I choose joy. I write the words, but they feel flat.

Speak them again.

I choose joy. I choose joyfulness. I choose a life that takes joy as its talisman, its hallmark. I choose a balanced life where serious does not rule with an iron fist, but sits lightly on a shimmering foundation of laughter and joy, of lightness and ease, of love. Which is joy.

See how naturally those words came? Soon the feelings and consequent actions will come just as naturally. Remember to choose joy. Acknowledge the joy that is already in your heart, that already finds expression through you. Don't punish yourself for the joy you cannot yet let in. Once you surrender to it, joy will bubble to the surface of your awareness like the sweet waters of an eternal spring. If the surface of that spring is still frozen, step onto it. Feel the ice crack and break under the weight of your love, under the power of your smile, under the joy of your heart. Melt the ice of self-denial. Break up the ice of self-punishment. Let the waters of joy, laughter and love bubble and burble to the surface, then flow, skip and play along their winding, circuitous stream.

Play. Do it not as work, not as growth, but for its own sake. Play and the growth will flow from it. Be a warrior for spirit, but a gentle warrior, a smiling warrior, a laughing knight. Let your heart release the spiritual prisoner and transform him into a laughing pilgrim.

A laughing pilgrim. I like that. I feel lighter already.

Choose joy. And joy will choose you. Let it swim freely through you just as you let these words swim freely onto the page. Think of fish dancing in the sea, of dolphins cavorting among the waves. Let these images guide you into the joy that is your birthright, the joy that is you.

Thank you.

Namaste.

Friday, February 14, 1997
DAWN

I nearly always close my eyes to experience these dialogues, even while writing. Longhand, the risk is that the resulting scrawl will be indecipherable. The risk on the computer, I discover today, is in deleting an entire dialogue by blindly hitting a wrong key sequence. The experience reminds me to not take this writing too seriously.

These writings are a means, not an end. They are a tool for your growth, a tool for your teaching. Don't tangle yourself up in the materialism of these words. Don't take them so seriously that they overshadow everything else. Don't take anything that seriously. Life is not meant to be taken that seriously. Life is not meant to be spent hidden behind a computer screen — eyes closed in meditation or not. Life is meant to be lived, to be lived in each moment.

These words may link you with your wisdom and divinity, but you do not need these words to link you with your wisdom and divinity. All you need resides within you and is immediately accessible from moment to moment. What you need — and what others will gain from these writings and this wisdom — comes from an authentic place of living, not from a place of need, addiction or hiding.

Go out into the world, as you prepare to do in leaving your Penetanguishene retreat. Carry these words and your heart-words from this place of hiding into the world. Be in (but not of) the world. Be in it where your words and your heart can have their greatest impact.

LATE EVENING

It's nearly midnight and I feel drawn to this blank page that I have been avoiding all evening. I have been feeling out of sorts since midway through a friend's visit here this afternoon. And now—

God, I hate this. I hate this bloated feeling. I hate myself for not being able to eat like a normal human being. I hate myself for hating myself. I hate my woundedness. I hate my fear. Perhaps I hate that most of all.

My fear. It never seems to go away. I never seem to be able to reach the bottom of it. There is always more and it always — most always — succeeds in debilitating me in some way...emotionally, physically or both. I hate it. I hate it. I hate it!

I sense my wisest self wanting me to write, "choose fearlessness." It might as well say, "Jump off the CN Tower[3] and you'll fly." Maybe it is possible, but I lack that depth of belief in this moment. The same holds true for the fear that grips me, grips me, grips me. Squeezes the air out of me. Makes it impossible for me to digest my food. Two small bowls of soup and a small salad: That's hardly gorging myself. But I feel as though I gorged myself à la Henry VIII. I feel like the anorexic who eats and eats and eats and then throws up. No, that's a bulimic. Whatever. I feel scared, out of control. I feel inadequate to the simplest of human functions after breathing: feeding myself. It ought to be so simple. I make it so complicated. I make everything so complicated. Then I punish myself. No compassion. No forgiveness. Why have I left no room for forgiveness? Why have I left no room for error? Why is it always self-denial and self-punishment?

Tonight my porch light burnt out and my flashlight died. It feels as though my inner light against the dark also shattered, leaving me vulnerable and at risk. I don't know what to do. I don't know what to feel, other than fear. I seem to be experiencing much and learning little.

---

3 A Toronto landmark that was then the world's tallest freestanding structure.

> Nonsense. You move at lightning speed. You learn at breathtaking pace. You are on the final stretch of this stage of your journey. The final stretch is always strewn with extra hazards. This is normal...and strengthening. You will come through this period. You do come through it. You fly through it.

Fly? It sure doesn't feel like flying. It feels more like crawling through mud and barbed wire...like some scene from a World War I movie.

> It is a sort of battlefield: a battlefield of love, a battlefield for love... for love of self. *Your*self. Love yourself as you deserve to be loved. Let that love flow through you. Let it heal you. It is no accident that you write about self-love and forgiveness.

Yes. Perhaps I needed to vent more than anything else. Right now I feel as though I need to sleep more than anything else.

> Then sleep. Sleep the sleep of the healed, of the held, of the wholed. Surrender into sleep, into the world of dreams. Surrender into love.

Saturday, February 15, 1997
PREDAWN

It takes an extra day, until Friday, for Toronto's Now *weekly to make it up north. So each Friday I pick up the latest edition and scour its roommates-wanted ads. Most weeks, I find nothing. This week is a blessed exception: "Vegetarian household committed to community seeks new addition." Will they take a dog? Lisa promises to consult her housemates. All I can do now is wait.*

Listen to the stillness. It's complete. The only sound is the scratch of my pen, of my heart-words falling from pen onto page. This is a blessed time of the day…despite my fear, despite my anxiety. Despite all my anguish, this is a blessed time of the day, these moments before dawn…as the first tangerine light spreads across the sky and illumines the world.

> Let it illumine your heart. Let it lighten your load, lighten your being. Let it wash away the fear.

I wish…I wish for strength.

> You have it. Recognize that and access it, not through any forced act of will but by the simple act of recognition, itself a form of letting. Let go your fear. Live in the present. Be filled with joy at this new day, at this new opportunity for growth, for love, for joy. Let joy override all else. Let joy overpower your fear.
>
> This moment, this day — these are all the now you have. Live them. Live them now. Live them in the now — consciously and with love. Self-love. Self-esteem. Self-respect.

I know why I'm anxious. It's because I'm waiting for Lisa to call about the house. I'm afraid of both a yes to Roxy and a no to Roxy, even though I know that whatever the answer, it will be for my highest good.

> You fear the future, yet the future is not important. Only one thing counts, ever: this instant, this breath. Hasn't that been shown you again and again?

Yes.

> Then remember it. Tomorrow may never come. Lisa's call may never come. Are you going to destroy this moment out of fear — for a future that cannot exist until it is present? For until it is present, it is only fantasy. Don't live your life in fantasy. Live it now. The only urgency is the urgency of now, the pressing matter of now. Nothing else matters. Nothing else exists.
>
> You have wished for the outcome that serves your highest good, not for specific outcomes. Now, learn to live with the uncertainty that must always follow. Learn to love that uncertainty, to derive strength from it. You might as well, for there is no certainty, except for the certainty of your innate wisdom and divinity…and the uncertainty that flows from them.

Thank you for these reminders, these gifts, this wisdom.

> The gifts are your gifts. The wisdom is your wisdom. The divinity is you. Acknowledge that.

It's hard some mornings…this morning.

> Say: "I feel my joy. I feel my power."

I feel my joy. I feel my power. It feels flat.

> Saying is part of making it so, of letting it be so, of letting it emerge into your life, into your heart. Feel your heart opening. See your heart opening. What do you see?

A white rose or lotus, unfurling its petals.

Your heart opens, so beautifully. Let it. Don't close it up again with worry. Don't worry about home. You carry your home within you. As for your "outer" home, it will find you. Trust, and all will be well, as all is well.

I do trust.

Then there is nothing to worry over. Worry is lack of trust. If you trust, there is never any room for worry.

I'm tired and shaky but somewhat revived. Still scared, but more grounded. Thank you, as always.

Namaste.

Sunday, February 16, 1997

EVENING

Lisa calls: The Pauline Avenue residents want to meet me and Roxy. Then a second call, this one from an anxious friend. As I offer him inspiration and encouragement, I know that my powerful words are as much for me as for him. The moment I hang up, I seize up in fear.

My own words of power: They terrify me. All that amazing truth expressed to Sam, all that amazing *me*, has tied me in knots. I'm afraid, afraid to be. I feel like a pretzel, with a knot at every twist. I want to let go, but I don't know how. I want to feel, but I don't know how. I do know how, but I'm scared. I'm scared of the power I expressed on that call. I'm scared of *my* power. I'm afraid, afraid I will harm someone...afraid I will harm myself. Afraid I'm not worthy. Just afraid.

> All you need, all you are, all the power, all the energy, all the healing, all the love, all the forgiveness, all the compassion, all the hope, all the help, all the holiness, all the wholeness: They all reside within you, in this moment. They *are* you. They are you at your wisest, at your most sacred, at your most divine. Do not fear them. Do not fear yourself. Be them. You have chosen to live your truth, and now you live it. You speak it and you live it. Let go all that holds you back from experiencing it, from expressing it, from accepting it.

I don't know how. I don't know what to do. I don't know how to un-seize myself from the grip of this sudden terror.

> There is nothing to do. There is only being. Be your *lieber Mann*, your beloved. Your divine. Your wisest self. That is all that is

ever asked of you. That is all you ever need ask of yourself. There is nothing simpler than being. Being is breathing. Being is listening. Being is sitting in the stillness of your heart. Being is waiting…waiting at the summit of the mountain that you, in all your courage, in all your heart, have scaled. Sitting. Waiting. Breathing. Being. Just being.

You make it sound so simple. It doesn't feel simple.

Only because you resist. Why resist when you know your resistance will break down, is breaking down? Your being here at this page in this moment speaks to that. Do not fear your power, for your power is a power for good, a power for love. Begin by loving yourself, by loving yourself as you have never loved anyone or anything before. Be that love. Express that love. Don't be afraid for all to see you in the expression of your love and your power. It is important that they see. It is part of your healing, and theirs. Just as these words you write in dialogue are part of your healing and will be part of theirs.

You are reluctant to claim these words as your own. You would prefer to call them "channeling" and to say that they come from outside you. They do not. Claim them. They are yours and always have been — an expression of your wisest self. They have always been a part of you, but you let them be hidden…hidden away until this great time of your healing, of your enlightenment.

Thank you. I needed to see those words on the page, even as I knew them…know them. Again, thank you. Thank me!

Well put. Namaste.

Tuesday, February 18, 1997

JUST AFTER MIDNIGHT

I feel calm, centered and in my power during the two hours Roxy and I spend with three of the five Pauline Avenue residents. But the moment I'm back in the car, I freak out and begin to eat. My choice of snack food may be healthy; my anxiety-provoked, obsessive eating is not.

I must be terrified. I scarfed down a muffin almost as soon as I left Pauline Avenue, then fists full of trail mix on the road, then toast when I got home, breaking my rule about bedtime snacks.

> There are no rules.

True. But I don't like to give in to my fears. I try not to stuff myself full of avoidance.

> For the most part you do admirably. Don't punish yourself. Acknowledge your lapse, resolve to do better next time and move on.

I don't need to punish myself. My heartburn is doing it for me.

> That is not punishment. It is your body gripping up with fear. It is okay to be afraid. What happened today on Pauline Avenue was big. What you did today was big. The life in community you opened yourself up to was enormous. Feel your fear. But don't neglect to praise your courage. Celebrate your audacity. Acknowledge your valor, your humor, your wit.

My wit?

> Your wit is part of your truth, as is your honesty. You touched Susan, Lisa and Roger today with your spirit, your truth, your

vulnerability and your wit. No one can remain untouched in the face of that. That alone is worthy of celebration. It does not matter whether you end up living there. You did good work.

I'm so scared.

Don't run from your fear. Don't run from your destiny.

I'm scared — of the commitment, of the intimacy, of the sharing.

You did it with Fred.

Not easily. And that was different.

Yes, but it has prepared you for this, just as your time alone in Penetanguishene has prepared you. You are ready for this next stage in your healing journey. That, too, scares you, doesn't it: the uncertainty that Toronto brings?

Yes, though I felt surprisingly at home in the house. And being back in the city felt so very right. Being back here feels right too. No, it feels safe.

Too safe?

Perhaps.

Is it time to shake things up a bit?

Perhaps, as much as I hate to admit it.

Trust the uncertainty. Trust the newness. Trust the rebirth about to happen. If the labor pains have begun, know that with each rebirth of yours they are of shorter duration and diminished intensity.

I'm exhausted. I don't think I can maintain my focus much longer... what little focus I have at this moment.

Then let it go. Embrace the night, as you embrace your fear. Embrace the uncertainty too. It heralds new and wondrous things. Now, rest your eyes and body — let your spirit speak to you through dream.

Thank you.

Namaste.

AFTERNOON

I don't know what to do about this fear that's burning a hole in my chest, in my heart. Heartburn.

There is nothing to do. Let your fear in. Feel the fear.

I want to heal that. I want to move past my fear. I don't want to give in to it. I don't want it getting in the way.

I sit quietly for a few minutes.

I hear crying, the tears of a boy who feels abandoned. He hides in a dark corner, afraid to come out. He doesn't feel pain. He is pain.

Take him in your arms and comfort him.

He runs as I approach. He's afraid, even of me.

I begin a dialogue with the boy, the boy who was and in some ways still is me.

I won't hurt you. I love you. I want to protect you from the pain, from the ravages of that pain. I want to father you and mother you. Trust me, little one. Trust me to carry you, to keep you safe.

I'm afraid.

I know you are. Me too. But together we can be so much braver than either one of us could be on his own. Together, we can step out into the world.

> I don't want to go out into the world. I want to hide.

Let me protect you. Let me hold you. I won't drop you. Not ever. I love you.

> I'm afraid...so afraid. I will be judged into oblivion.

That was the past. I can protect you now. All I could do before was hide, with you. I'm stronger now. We both are. But if you don't trust your strength, trust mine.

> I want to, but I'm afraid.

Wanting means you are more than halfway to courage. I have kept you safe until now, haven't I?

> Y-e-e-es.

Then take one tiny step — not a big leap, just one tiny step into that little bit of more trust you need to cross the bridge. Let me carry you, beautiful boy. Come with me. Grow with me. Do you understand what I'm trying to say?

> That you love me, that I'm safe within that love.

Yes.

The little boy dissolves, and I am back in conversation with the Divine, with my wisest self.

My heartburn has lessened.

> You have begun to face your fear. As you face it, it loses its power over you. It diminishes until it disappears into the void, into that great emptiness you fear so much. It is going. It will soon be gone. Trust. Trust, and all will be well.

I love you.

> Then you love yourself. Try saying that.

I love myself. It's still hard to say.

> Does it get easier?

Yes, and I'm grateful for that.

> You move through turbulent, earthquaking changes right now. But you have all the courage and fortitude you need, the same courage and fortitude you convinced Sam on Sunday that he had. Let the words you used to inspire him and others inspire you as well.

I choose fearlessness. I choose my strength. I choose to live my truth. I choose to carry that truth out into the world. I choose to protect those parts of me that need protection. I feel fear but I am not fear.

> Well spoken. You do well. Acknowledge that. And when you receive praise, as you did this afternoon from Odette, don't be so dismissive.

Was I dismissive?

> You were. Less than in the past, but still dismissive. Accept the praise and gratitude. You deserve it.

Thank you.

> Thank yourself! Know that this heartburn will pass, just as this fear will pass. Know, too, that you will emerge from the fire restored, renewed and strengthened.

Again, thank you.

> Namaste.

EARLY EVENING

This is about letting go...about being afraid to let go...to let go the controls that make me feel safe, that have made me feel safe. This is about trust, about trusting that I will be safe once those controls are lifted. I know the safety was an illusion, but I felt safe in that illusion. Now I'm being asked me to throw it all away...to live without a net.

> You are asking yourself. You are choosing. You want this.

I do. I want this experience. I want this healing. I want this community. I crave this community. I want to connect deeply in ways more meaningful than I ever have before. How can I want it so deeply and fear it so profoundly all at the same time?

> Change. It is calling on you to change. You are calling on you to change. Yet that word, that concept — "change" — is illusion. You are not changing your essential nature. You are rediscovering that essential nature. You are rediscovering your authentic self. You are rediscovering your wisest self. You are seeking to leave behind your separation, your separateness. You are seeking to reclaim your place in unity, in wholeness, in holiness.

So why do I fight myself over it? Why can't I move toward it with grace and joy, with ease and gratitude?

> This is part of the learning, the growth, the journey. Like Dorothy in Oz, you cannot just click your heels three times and find yourself home. You must first travel the journey, the healing path that carries you home.
>
> That you acknowledge your heart's desire in this is a major accomplishment. It is a milestone worthy of celebration and praise. Remember how you could not want to teach until you were doing it? Now you are able to acknowledge and embrace

your desires. Yes, you resist. But that resistance is little more than a shadow of its former self. It shrinks and pales yet more from instant to instant.

Will it ever be gone?

It will vanish in the letting go.

I want to let go. I want to be free. I want to cut away the chains that bind me to a past that is no longer relevant. I want to meet my destiny. I don't want to fight. I want to be free.

You are free. You have always been free. Acknowledge your freedom, and as you do you will live that freedom more and more. Continue to let go, and the mending will accelerate. Come home, home to your self, to the spirit of love within you, to the wisdom and divinity that is you.

I do. I come home. Because I want to. Because I need to. Because there is no other true path for me. Thank you.

EVENING

I have been accepted into the Pauline Avenue house — not in my first choice of room, which would have been spacious and bright with natural light, but in a dark, womb-like space that, like my house on Champlain Road, would never have been my conscious first choice as a home.

Help! I'm having an anxiety attack. There are so many reasons to feel panicked, and I'm not sure which is the true one. Am I scared because I have decided to move in? Is it because I'll be in a tiny, dark room that is one of the noisiest in the house? Am I confused because it feels so right to move in, regardless of which room I take? Because it does, and that confuses me in much the same way as when I saw 296 Champlain Road and recognized its rightness, even as my logical mind screamed "No!" What am I getting myself into? What will it be like to be spending so much time in that darkness?

> You spoke wisely and true when you told Roger that Pauline Avenue for you would be about the people, not about rooms and furniture. Your room is in your heart. Your home is in your heart.
> Regardless, maybe you will not be spending as much time in your room as you think. Maybe this will ensure you don't. Perhaps it will force you out into the open, into the common, shared areas. Maybe this is about creating a cozy space rather than an open space. Maybe it is about things you cannot yet begin to see. Follow your heart, as you do, and let go all expectation and doubt. Don't predicate the future based on the past. This is a new way of doing and being. Let it be as it needs to be, and it will be as you need it to be, in ways you cannot now imagine.

It's hard to let go the expectations, the past-based wants.

> By agreeing to take the room, you have already done that. You have let go expectations. You have entered into the unknown, willingly and trustingly. With love and with trust.

My heartburn is back. The pain in my side is back.

> Fear. Clinging, gripping fear. Let go. Let go and all will be well. Let go into trust. Let go into love.

I know this is the right place. It's just—

> It's just that it is new. It is change. It not at all what you thought you wanted. That's okay. Follow your heart, as you do. Embrace the uncertainty, as you do. Live in trust and surrender, as you do. Embrace the miracle, as you do.

I embrace the miracle. I choose fearlessness. I surrender to the light that shines my way through the dark. To my light. To my power. I trust my power. I trust the empowerment that allowed me to say yes to Pauline Avenue despite all that might have once stood in my way. I am determined to live in the present. *This* is my present. This is my life.

>The healing journey continues.

I celebrate it. And I'm scared shitless!

>You acknowledge your feelings. You let yourself feel your fear. It will pass.

Thank you. I'm still feeling shaky, but I have no doubt that my decision was the right one. Despite my uncertainty at a logical, left-brain level, I know it is right. I know it is true. I know it as my truth.

>So be it.

Thank you.

>Namaste.

Wednesday, February 19, 1997
MORNING

Just as my moving-to-Nova Scotia timeline rapidly collapses from five years to five months[4], my return-to-Toronto timeline also swiftly folds in on itself: Instead of my planned March 10 departure, I realize that there is no reason not to leave a week earlier...as my exodus accelerates.

I have decided: I will move into Pauline Avenue on March 3. I now leave a week earlier than planned. In less than two weeks! Am I ready for this?

> You are ready, readier than you have ever been. You have completed in Penetanguishene what you came to do. It is time to move on. It is time to let this life die and be born again into the new one. You are ready.

When I woke this morning, the fear was gone. The heartburn was gone. The panic was gone.

> You faced your fear. You didn't run from it. You entered into it. In doing so, you stripped it of its power. That does not mean that things will always be easy or free from fear. But you opened your arms to this particular demon and you befriended it, transformed it and recycled it. Now it is no longer a demon. Now it is on the side of the angels.

I'm incredulous about the sudden shift to March 3. I feel almost like I felt that day when Nova Scotia went from being five years away to only a year away...that was before it collapsed again to five months. I don't know what else to say but "Oh my God!" It feels as though the future is opening up right before my eyes and it's studded

---
4 See January 6 (evening) entry.

with brilliant lights. It's amazing, exciting, miraculous, wondrous, awesome. I'm grateful, ever so grateful. Thank you.

> Thank yourself. You have chosen this. You have made it happen by letting it happen, by letting yourself let it happen. Pull up anchor, start the engines and go.

I'm going. I'm smiling. I'm grinning, oh so broadly. I'm ready.

> That you are! Namaste.

EVENING

I felt so clear this morning...so exultant. Now I'm anxious all over again. Not as anxious as yesterday, but I don't want to be afraid. I want that excitement back, that amazed, amazing, wondrous wonder.

> It will return. For now, acknowledge your fear. Visit with it. Befriend it. Ask it to tea. You recoil at the thought?

I guess I do.

> Stop seeing fear as your enemy. It is no enemy. It is a frightened friend, a vulnerable friend. Don't run from it. Respect it as you would respect a friend. Hear it out as you would hear out a friend. Do that and you will move through and past your fear — back to exultation.

Is it that simple?

> Always.

I don't want to write this...

> Do.

My fear is dumb. It's weak. It's sniveling. I want no part of it. I don't want that fear as a friend.

> Your fear is part of you. You cannot dismiss it and denigrate it without dismissing and denigrating part of yourself, part of your divinity.

I just want it to go away.

> Then treat it with respect. Treat it with dignity. Treat it with love. Treat yourself with love. All of you: the fear as much as the exultation. If you are to feel your feelings, you must be prepared to feel all of them — the joy, the pain, the fear, the exultation. Feel the fear. Feel it fully. Then let it go and it will go. As it has before.

And then came back.

> Diminished.

True.

> Each time it will be diminished yet further until it exists not at all. There is too much fear within you — a history of great fear — for it to disappear overnight. It is a process and a journey. You live that process and journey with great courage. Acknowledge that. Celebrate that. Don't punish yourself for feeling. Don't punish yourself over feelings that are genuine, that are real, that are true. Never punish the truth. It is too precious for that.

I think I know why I'm afraid. It's the realization of how quickly this is happening. This life ends and the new one begins in less than two weeks.

> You have made that choice. You can choose otherwise. You can choose to stay longer here.

To do what? No, I must leave when it is time to leave. My time here is over. It is time to let winter die so a new spring can emerge — my new spring.

> Yes. Now, tell your fear you understand why it feels as it does. Tell your fear you love and respect it. Acknowledge the service your fear has provided in the past. Express your gratitude, then let it go. Let it go and move into the new. Move into the know. Move into the now.

To my fearful selves: I'm sorry if you feel that I have treated you badly. It's just that you remind me of the past, and I don't want to go back to that place. I know that place feels safer for you. That safety is illusion. I can protect you now — if you let me, if you trust me. Come with me into the new, into this new adventure. You don't need fear to protect you anymore. Do you trust me?

> Yes.

Will you journey with me?

> Okay.

I feel the fear and let it go. I experience the fear and let it go. I embrace the fear and let it go. I don't run anymore. I am not afraid, not even of fear. I love myself — all parts of myself. I don't feel much better.

> You are doing fine. You are on the right track.

It all feels so disjointed, so rambling — so confused.

> Just say what you need to say, be what you need to be. You don't need those old ways anymore. They are of the past and you are of the present. Be in the present. Be present — in your fear as in your courage. In your anxiety as in your exultation.

I think I need to stop. I think I need to take the next step. I need to call Roger and let him know I'm coming a week early.

> Go. Take the next step toward your destiny, take the next step on your road toward healing and enlightenment.

I set pen and paper aside and make the call.

Thursday, February 20, 1997

DAWN

I'm overwhelmed, both by the thought of all I have to do before leaving and by the idea of doing none of it — or at least the least of minimums.

> This is a dying time, not a building time. Respect that. Respect winter's last breath by entering into its silence, by embracing its uncertainty, by opening into its darkness. Don't try to mold certainty out of uncertainty. There is no need to make decisions right now, about anything. Do what needs to be done, the absolute minimum. Life will be so different for you at the other end that planning for it now is pointless. Don't worry about what to bring and what to leave behind. Don't worry about the new house and its dynamics. You have made your commitment. You have chosen your date. Leave it at that. Let everything else percolate at the edges of your consciousness. It will sort itself out.

Thank you.

> Respect the deaths that move through you, and the new lives will unfold like a million-million rainbow petals, shimmering in the dew-dipped dawn.

EVENING

Rain is falling, washing away the old, cleansing away the dirt, melting the ice…the ice in my heart. Why am I still so afraid to be in my heart?

> Your fear has kept you from your heart, from yourself. But that was then. Don't let your fear keep you away now.

I keep hearing the word "despair."

> Despair is from the old life. Let that life go.

There is so much I want to let go of. Why is it still so difficult? You'll say it isn't. You'll say to unclench. My fingers are clenched so tightly it's as if I would need a crowbar to pry them open. And I feel that gripping in my chest as the acid backs up, as the bile rises.

> You feel your fear.

I'm tired of hearing that.

> What are you afraid of?

Loss of control. What do I get for giving up this illusion I cling to so ferociously?

> You gain back yourself, your self-respect, your life.

I feel doubt.

> Do you not trust?

Most of the time, yes. At this instant? I don't know. I'm tired. I have heartburn.

> Give yourself time.

What time? I have to be out of here in eleven days.

> There are no "have to's." If you are not ready you can delay. You will be ready. You will be more than ready; you will be impatient to leave. This final hurdle, this fear, is the last gasping struggle of the old. Let it die. Don't struggle. Let it be. Let yourself be. Just let.

I want to eat. I want to stuff myself.

Yet you don't. Do you celebrate that?

No. I'm too busy wanting to eat. What do I do? What do I do to ease this pain? What do I do to find peace?

> Let peace find you. Don't fight the pain. Be with it and it will lose its power.

Will I feel like this every day? It's exhausting.

> Struggle always is. Don't punish yourself for your feelings. You have courage, tremendous courage. And you are buttressed by phenomenal faith. Faith in miracles. Faith in yourself. Faith in your wisdom and divinity.

I don't feel that faith right now. Or that wisdom. Or that divinity.

> It is there, or you would not be able to do what you do. You would not be able to let go.

Am I letting go?

> Of course you are. Let the dying happen. Let it be. Let yourself be.

Words, words, words. I'm sick of the same words. Let me write something different, something new, something that will work, something that will neutralize this acid of anxiety that eats at my insides.

> There are no new words, only ancient truths.

I feel so helpless.

> Yet you are imbued with enviable strength. See the strength that others see in you. It is there.

I'm just so tired. Of everything. If I can't eat, I want to hide. I'm sick and tired of the same bloody counsel. I want a cure for this morass, this painful, acidic— God, I'm tired.

> Tired of fighting?

Yes.

> Then surrender. Surrender to your own divinity.

I can't. I'm afraid.

> You can and you do. You can and you will. Trust. Trust in the power of your soul, of your heart, of your divinity. Trust in the power of your connection to universal wisdom, to the oneness that is all.

I'm losing my focus. This is rambling over old territory.

> Then let it go and sit. Let it go and be in the silence, in the stillness of the night.

The phone rings. I take the call.

In talking to Odette just now, I remember two things I told her about my journey to help reassure her about hers. One, there are no good days and no bad days, just difficult and easy days…and the difficult days are just as good as the easy ones. Two, it's okay to be tired and cranky. Big things are moving through me, so it's okay to feel whatever I feel. It's okay to *feel*. It's okay to be me at this moment in time. It's okay. I'm okay. I will get through this.

> Of course you will.

Thank you.

> The gift is yours. Bless it and yourself. Namaste.

Friday, February 21, 1997
AFTERNOON

I'm feeling overwhelmed, almost assaulted by my fear-filled projections of what awaits me in Toronto. It's such a massive change, such a massive abdication of control that I don't know that I can cope. I'm panicking. I don't know what to do. Doing nothing seems only to exacerbate the panic. I can't go on like this.

> You won't. Let go. Let go the fear. Let go the projections. Feel your panic. Write your panic, as you do. Writing, for you, is centering, grounding, focusing, directing, guiding, supporting, reassuring, comforting, opening. It is your power at work. *Your* power. That is important to acknowledge.

I also feeling the finality of this: I put through my change of address at the post office today. That makes it feel so real, so concrete. March 3 is only ten days away. A week from Monday my life turns upside-down. Nothing will be the same again.

> This is an important threshold for you. Acknowledge that. Respect that. Allow yourself to move toward it with compassion and love. Don't judge your fear. It is not bad. It just is. It will pass. It already passes through you. You are shedding an old skin. Let it happen. Be in the fear if that is what you are feeling. Don't run from it. Just be in it and be with it.

I'm doing my best, but my best doesn't seem good enough.

> It is. Respect the magnitude of this change. Don't be so hard on yourself. Don't expect so much. Don't expect perfection. If you feel fear, allow that fear, without judgment. Choose fearlessness when you can, but always feel what you are feeling and honor

yourself by honoring those feelings. Honor, too, your strength and courage.

You will be fine. You will shine. You will explode with light, with streams of iridescence, until the night is clothed in brilliant light — the brilliant light that you are, the shining beacon of wisdom and vulnerability that you are. Your wisdom and vulnerability are precious. Don't hide them. Don't mask them. Don't build new walls around them. Be them. Be yourself.

Thank you, as always. I wish I could find more comfort — more immediate comfort — in these words.

That will come. For now, take it as it comes. Be as it is. Just be.

Saturday, February 22, 1997
EVENING

Silent night. No sounds from the road. No sounds from the Emerys. Nothing but my breath and the rasp of pen against page. Will I ever experience this stillness again? This peace?

> You will find it in your heart, where it always is. The idea is not to need external silence, but to be able to tap into inner silence whenever and wherever. At those moments the outside world will not matter.

It's so easy to be distracted, even here where the silence is nearly always complete.

> Let the distractions be. Let them come and go, just as you let stray thoughts and nagging worries come and go — in meditation and, increasingly, outside of meditation. Do the same with the external noises that will surround you in your new space. Living in that cauldron of humanity is about living in the world, with all its noise and distraction, while remaining connected to your inner stillness...while remaining connected to this wisdom, which is your wisdom, to these words which are— After all these months, you still cannot quite accept these words as your own?

The voice — it doesn't feel as though it's mine.

> It is the same voice that speaks wise words of inspiration and reassurance to your friends. These are your words. This is your *author*ity. Don't disempower yourself. Claim your expression. Claim your truth. Shout it from the rooftops.

Publish and be damned?

Publish and be blessed.

You're right. I'm sorry.

Don't apologize. Be.

These words, my words...they're wise. It's easier to live them than to— I'm smiling because that's not what I meant to write. I meant to write, "It's easier to write them than to live them."

> It is easy to live them. Open your heart and you live them already. It is not about living them in perfection. That would be impossible. It is about living them in your humanity, which is as much your divinity as your imperfection. It is about living them as you are. As you do that, the "as you are" grows and expands in consciousness and into an ability to live them even more fully. It is a journey, a growing. It is a "getting there" not a being there. For each arrival is but a new beginning.

I think I need to sit in stillness for a while. Or maybe I need a couple of good screams. I'm still having some difficulty assimilating the symbolically big things I did today around the move.

> You are alone. No one will hear. Scream. Shout. Shout out your anger. Shout out your fear. Shout out your rage. Shout out your joy. Stand up and shout. It is all about release.

I scream as loud and as long as I can. Roxy, accustomed to my odd behavior by now, opens one eye then shuts it back again in sleep.

Now what?

You say.

I feel more stillness. I feel less agitation. My throat is sore.

> You need to learn how to shout from your gut not your throat. Apart from that, well done! Wasn't it good to get it out, to let it out, to let go?

Even if I don't do it fully.

> You judge. You did what you did, what you could do in that moment. Celebrate the accomplishment. Don't punish the perceived lack.

I celebrate my accomplishments and achievements. I love myself. I choose love. I choose life. I don't feel very life-affirming at this moment. I feel tremendous fatigue, intense fatigue. I just want to sleep.

> Whatever is happening in this moment is whatever you need. Don't fight it. Sleep, if sleep is what calls to you.

Thank you. I will.

Monday, February 24, 1997
EVENING

I'm having a rough time. I know what I'm afraid of: the move and the possibility of my first Pathlights client. I just don't know what to do about it. If I have to write "don't do, be" one more time, I'll scream.

> Then scream.

Very funny.

> There is no doing that needs doing. There is no running from being, from being in your fear so you can move through it and past it — as you wrote today in your new Pathlights brochure, as you will tell your clients.

I hate that word. I'm not offering a product. I'm offering a life — the keys to a life, a road map of sorts, a "path light." These aren't clients or students or patients. What are they?

> Fellow travelers. Fellow journeyers. Fellow questers. Whatever you call them (and "clients" is not a bad word), whether or not the referral pans out, you are ready for them, readier than you have ever been. Embrace your readiness and embrace yourself — your wisest self, your divine self, your power, your healing power, your power for good.

And my fear?

> Embrace that too, and it will pass as yesterday's did. As tomorrow's will.

I'm anxious and depressed and frightened.

Don't fight it. Be it.

That sounds so simple, yet so difficult.

Surrender control. All control. Surrender to your highest good, to your highest wisdom, to your divinity. Surrender to life, to your life. Put your pen down and surrender.

Wednesday, February 26, 1997
EVENING

I am barely in Nova Scotia six weeks when, during a meditative walk, I sense with increasing clarity and alarm that despite all the synchronicity that has lured me to rural Yarmouth County, I can expect to return to Toronto. I have a similar realization on a similar walk this afternoon — not about my return to Toronto, but about a further exodus, from Toronto.

I'm in a state of shock, so stunned by what I sensed this afternoon that it has taken me this long to be able to sit still long enough to write about it. I haven't even made it to Toronto and I'm leaving it again? Talk about speed! Talk about fear. I don't want to be afraid of this. I want to be excited. But the speed…the speed. I knew to expect accelerated speeds, but I never expected this.

> You ain't seen nothin' yet!

Gee, thanks. I thought this was supposed to reassure me.

> Your power is intact. How is that for reassurance? Your power soars on eagle's wings. How is that for reassurance? The time has come for you to take your word out into the world. How is that for reassurance? It reassures you that what you will gain from your experience on Pauline Avenue will move through you in record time.

Right now it feels like I'll leave Pauline Avenue after seven months. Not that long ago, it felt as though I would be on Pauline for a year. Then, I didn't see myself leaving Toronto at all after that. Could this timeline collapse yet more, like it did with Nova Scotia?

> Absolutely. Anything is possible. But don't get caught up in timelines. Be present. Know what lies ahead. Know also that it is changeable.

But it will change in favor of speeding up not slowing down.

> Likely, but not certainly. All there is for you to do is to stay grounded in the present moment and trust.

I do. I guess I'm still not quite able to assimilate it: heartburn again.

> The assimilation will happen, quickly. All will happen quickly. Fasten your seatbelt.

It's still fastened from last time! Now what?

> Now, nothing. Carry these words into your sleep, into your dreams, into the night. Let sleep transform and reinvigorate it… and you. Then enter into your new day refreshed, rejuvenated and ready to carry forward with your plans. You know what you need to do. You know what you want to do, what your heart desires. You will do it.

I will. Somehow, I will. Thank you.

> Namaste.

LATE EVENING

A phone conversation with a Toronto friend leaves me feeling insecure and uncertain after he insists that I am living too much from intuition and not enough from logic.

I feel put down. I feel defensive. What if Paul is right?

> Only you can know what is right for you. You know that Paul speaks from a place of his own insecurity. Don't buy into that.

Maintain your grounding, your centeredness, your knowingness, your truth. Let his words slide off you, for nothing he said was about you. This is not the last time you will be challenged. When that happens, listen to your challenger, have compassion for him or her, and then live your life as you know in your heart of hearts it desires and demands to be lived. Live *your* path, not anyone else's. Live it and embody it.

Thank you.

Namaste.

Thursday, February 27, 1997

MORNING

I'm still haunted by last night's phone call.

> Let it go. Don't obsess about it. Leave Paul to his journey and continue to surrender to yours. Leave Paul to experience his demons of distrust and continue to leave yours behind. Bless him. Have compassion for him. But let it go. Let him go, if you must. You will encounter far more serious doubt from others in the months and years ahead. Practice being strong, being strong within yourself. Practice grounding yourself in your truth, in your wisdom, in your knowingness.

Thank you. I still feel shaky…tired…lethargic — fearful.

> The letting go continues: letting go of expectations. It is important, that. No expectations. Empty slate.

Then why these inner sensings about the future, about what happens after Pauline Avenue?

> Preparation.

Like my "early warning" in Nova Scotia about Toronto?

> Precisely. Adjustment time. Assimilation time. That can be important when things move quickly, as they do.

Boy, do they ever. You weren't kidding about that one. Thank you. I do feel better.

> You are strong. You are wise. You are beautiful. Know that. Live that. Be empowered by that. You are on your way!

Friday, February 28, 1997

EVENING

My final evening of solitary silence before I leave for Toronto. Tomorrow I am to be farewell-brunched and farewell-supped. Then... Then, the unknown. I get butterflies in my stomach at the thought.

> You are a butterfly. Delicate but strong. Animated but serene. Emergent into life, your life, the life you were meant to live, are called to live.

Desire to live.

> Good. Good for you to say that.

I have nothing to say tonight. Nothing to ask. The silence envelopes me. The darkness surrounds me. The void is within and without. The new beckons and the old dies away. I am in awe — of this process, of this path, of this journey.

> It is right to be awed. Be awed as well by your gifts: the gift to touch the souls of men, the hearts of men, the gift to reawaken sleeping spirits, the gift of unity, the gift of healing. Use them wisely. Use them well. Enter into this new adventure emboldened, enlightened, alive and a-love. Enter into it with peace and grace. Enter into it with joy.

Oh, God. Heartburn.

> It will pass. Your fear of what comes grips you in this moment. It will loosen its grip when it sees you mean it no harm. Nor does it mean you any harm. It seeks to protect. You can protect now,

with your truth, with your faith, with your love. They protect you. They are you.

I have nothing to ask, nothing to say, only to thank the divine words, wisdom and treasures that have sustained me through these five months and that have empowered me to move forward.

You are the words. You are the wisdom. You are the treasure.

I'm still only beginning to see that.

That awareness will expand as you let it, as you let go the old self-hatreds, the old wounds. Go, then, and be, speak, broadcast and publish your truth. Shout it from the rooftops. Let all hear and see you. Let all learn from you. Open your heart. Open your heart and be. Namaste.

Blessed Transformation

Every ending is also a new beginning. Every beginning is the first step toward a new ending. Thus, the spiral of life continues, from one blessed transformation to the next...

Monday, March 3, 1997
MORNING

Today is the day. What a night it has been leading up to it: a night of more dreams than sleep. So many dreams. Dreams of parts of me that cling like Velcro and won't leave or let go. Dreams of driving on the ice in winter, where the only way to be safe, to have any control, is to have no control, to shift into neutral. Dreams of living in community. Now what?

> Now, be. Now, do. Now, become. Now, ready yourself. Now, move into this new life you yourself have chosen and prepared. Surrender into it. Unclench your mind. Open your heart. Open to the changes, to the new life, to the blessed transformation.

Blessed transformation: I like that, better than the heartburn that plagued me last night. What a hopeful, helpful, loving phrase. What a joyous image.

> That is where you are. That is what you are and what you are about. That is your gift — to yourself and as a catalyst for others. Welcome yourself to this new turning on the road of life, the path of light. Your path of light. Travel that road. Be that journeyer, that quester — for yourself and for the world.

I do. I be. I am. Thank you.

Namaste.

Afterword

Days before leaving Penetanguishene, I took Roxy for a farewell walk along the white moonscape of snow and ice that is the beach at the bottom of the Sixteenth Concession Road. It was a luminous, frosty afternoon, an hour before sunset, the perfect moment to mark an ending. My cycle of hibernation, heart-healing, foundation-building and strengthening had passed and it was time to say a grateful adieu as I released into another new beginning, another rebirth.

More than seventeen years have passed since that walk and since the final namaste of the final dialogue of this book. In that heartbeat of time, worlds have birthed, died and been reborn — worlds I never expected to experience, worlds I never expected to shift as earthquakingly as they did.

To my surprise, I remained on Toronto's Pauline Avenue barely three months before I found myself on the exodus I had foreseen, once more traveling a road of surrender in uncharted directions. This time no fixed destination called me, only a westward pull whose siren force drew me across Ontario, into the United States and onto a three-month, ten-state odyssey that finally landed me amidst the spirited red rocks of Sedona, Arizona.

One exodus and blessed transformation followed the next over the ensuing years, carrying me from Sedona to Hawaii and back again; through marriage, fatherhood and divorce; along another open-ended road odyssey ten times the duration of the first; and into far-from-settled sojourns in Los Angeles and New Mexico, where I now pen these closing words.

I penned and published many more words through those years

of journeying. I finally completed *The MoonQuest*, such a source of anxiety during my Georgian Bay retreat, and I wrote its *StarQuest* and *SunQuest* sequels, all of which appear to be destined for a new life of their own, as feature films. I also published four books for writers, a memoir (aptly titled *Acts of Surrender*) and now, at last, these *Dialogues*. If Pathlights never took the form I expected, I discovered that it was never destined to be a physical center. Rather it was and is a heart center, my heart center. It lives within me and lies at the core of everything I write, teach, speak and live.

Nearly two decades after the challenging months chronicled on these pages, healing and transformation continue to move through me — not always easily and not always without fear. But the resistance weakens with each surrender, the fear dissolves more quickly with each act of trust and the rewards of my unconditional commitment to this way of being never cease to astound me.

In *The MoonQuest*, Toshar is reminded that "there is no end to the quest for those who choose to live the journey." It was true for him, it is true for me and it is true for us all when we listen to the voice of our heart and follow the path of our highest wisdom wherever it takes us. For wherever it takes us is always in the direction of wholeness, enlightenment, truth and love.

May you and I and all continue to travel that path in joy and surrender and in harmony with the divinity that is the birthright of each of us and all of us and all Creation.

Namaste
Mark David Gerson
October 2014

Dialogues with Your Divine

A Guide to Launching a Conversation with Your Wisest Self

You might think, in reading these dialogues, that my experiences were unique, that I was gifted with singular access to some sort of special wisdom.

It's not true.

I am no more powerful than you are. I am no more intuitive than you are. My potential is no vaster than yours. Nor is my wisest self any more committed to me than yours is to you. We are all wired to our divine nature. We all share the same emotional, spiritual and creative DNA. We all have equal access to the font of universal wisdom that resides in equal measure within each of us.

The key, as I was reminded frequently during my time in Penetanguishene, is to abandon the mind-centered controls that keep us locked in a prison of logic and unbelief. The key is to open our hearts to our infinite nature. The key is to listen, trust and surrender.

The Muse Stream technique I employed in these dialogues is not the only way to touch that inner realm where our wisdom and divinity reside. But it is a method that has proven effective for both me and my students over the years, so I am happy to share it with you here.

If you have read any of my books for writers or attended any of my creativity workshops, you will recognize much of what follows. If you haven't, know that this is not a rule-bound technique. Rather, it is a series of guidelines that I encourage you to play with, adapt and make your own, altering them as your needs and circumstances change.

To quote from my book *The Voice of the Muse: Answering the Call to Write*, "Write and let the words flow from your pen onto the page. Write and let the spirit of who you are emerge onto the page. All those things will happen the moment you unlock the gates that have kept the words, ideas, thoughts and feelings dammed up inside you. The Muse Stream frees you to allow that flow to happen. How? By training you to keep writing — through doubts, hesitation, fear and (seeming) unknowingness."

"Seeming" unknowingness? Absolutely, for the wisdom and guidance you seek has never left you and never will. It is for you to open your mind and heart to what is already there. It is for you to surrender...to you!

How to Free Your Wisest Self onto the Page

These are guidelines, not rules. Feel free to adapt them in whatever way feels most relevant and appropriate. Just remember that the goal is to let go all control of the process and to trust your intuition and inner sensings, both in terms of how you approach the experience and how you view the results.

- Have pen and paper, tablet or laptop handy, or sit as comfortably as you can at your desktop computer.

- Settle into a physical, emotional and spiritual state of stillness. If you have a meditation practice, do whatever you normally do to get into a receptive space. If not, close your eyes and sit quietly, focusing on your breath to quiet your mind. Use music, aromatherapy, crystals, yoga or ritual if you find any or all of these to be helpful. You can also use the "Meet Your Wisest Self" meditation on the next page to both relax you and guide you through the experience. (If you are unable to still your mind, don't worry about it. Writing your mind chatter will give it voice and, ultimately, silence it.)

- Write the first thought that comes to mind. It can be a question or feeling. It can be a statement of praise or complaint. It can be the voice of your inner critic, your fear or your inner child. It can be nattering mind noise. Whatever it is, write your side of the conversation, then let a response emerge spontaneously onto the page. Don't look for an answer. Don't think about an answer. *Let* the answer.

- The key, in both sides of your dialogue, is to write without stopping, to write without thinking, to write without correcting spelling, punctuation or grammar, to write without censoring or second-guessing, to write through and past any judgment or fear, to write in a morning-pages, stream-of-consciousness sort of way...to write on what I call in my books for writers the "Muse Stream." I call it that because I believe that when we surrender to the experience unconditionally, the words pour through us as effortlessly as water in a free-flowing stream.

- If you get stuck, and you may, remember the free-association technique I describe in my December 23 entry or simply repeat the last word or sentence you were able to write freely; keep repeating it until the flow returns, and it will. In either case, refocus your attention on your breath: If you are stuck in your dialogue you may be stuck in your breath.

- Write for as long as you feel the need to and then a little longer after that. The wisest words and deepest truths often emerge after we think we're done.

- If, when you're finished writing, you feel doubtful, cynical, judgmental or mistrustful of what has emerged, don't read it right away. Instead, set your writing aside for at least an hour. Take a walk or do something else unrelated to this experience. Then, when you feel able to look at what you have written uncritically and without judgment, read it with an open heart and mind to discover what messages your Wisest Self has for you.

Read more about the Muse Stream in any of my books for writers.

Meet Your Wisest Self: A Guided Meditation

Record this meditation for playback, get a friend to read it to you (and then return the favor) or get into a quiet space and read it to yourself slowly and receptively, following its directions and suggestions.

If you prefer a professionally guided approach, I have recorded a version that's nearly identical to what follows. It's titled "Meet Your Muse" and it's one of the tracks on my album "The Voice of the Muse Companion: Guided Meditations for Writers." Here's how to access it:

- Stream the individual track or the complete album for free as a subscriber to Apple Music, YouTube Music or Amazon's Music Unlimited.
- Download the individual track from Amazon or Apple Music.
- Download the full "Voice of the Muse Companion" album from my website (www.markdavidgerson.com/books), Apple Music, Amazon or CD Baby.

Relax. Close your eyes. Get into a comfortable position. Let your shoulders drop. And drop some more.

Take a few deep breaths, breathing in calm and quiet, breathing out fears, fatigue, stress. You're relaxed but alert. Awake and aware. Moving into a quiet place. A deep place. A place of freedom, vision, awakening.

In your mind's eye, see a door. A beautifully crafted door. Handcrafted. A work of art. Perhaps it's a new door, newly discovered. Perhaps it's ancient, as old as time, just waiting for you to rediscover it.

See it or sense it…however you see it or sense it.

This is your doorway of inner vision. Walk up to it. Run your hand over it. Feel its texture…its richness…its depth.

As you touch the door, it swings open. The door to your inner vision will always swing open at your touch…if you let it.

You are the key.

Now the door swings open and you step across the threshold. Into a wondrous place. Perhaps you recognize this place. Perhaps it's new. Whatever you see or sense and however you see or sense it is perfect, perfect for you, in this moment.

See or sense this place, this wondrous place. See or sense it fully, using all your senses. What does it look like? What colors do you see? How is the light? Do you hear any sounds? Smell any smells? Reach out and touch something. Feel its texture. What is the spirit of this place? What does it feel like, to you?

Now, coming toward you through this wondrous place, coming toward you bathed in light, is your Wisest Self. The essence of your divinity. The being that, in this moment, embodies your purest energy, that font of wisdom, inspiration and revelation that we all have within us.

This is yours. Unique to you.

However it manifests, whatever you see, sense or feel of it, is right for you. In this moment.

Open your mind and heart. Allow it to come to you in whatever form it comes, recognizing that its form can change from moment to moment, mood to mood, dialogue to dialogue.

There is no right or wrong image, right or wrong way. There is only the way you see or sense, and what you see and sense. And it's perfect. For you.

What does your Wisest Self look like? Feel like to you?

See or sense it fully. Again, use all your physical senses — sight, touch, smell, taste, sound. And your intuitive senses — feeling, spirit, essence.

Your Wisest Self now stands before you, and you greet each other in whatever way feels right, taking all the time you need.

Now, you and your Wisest Self begin a special dialogue.

Perhaps your Wisest Self has a message for you. Perhaps you have questions for your Wisest Self — questions about a specific issue or situation in your life, questions about how you are feeling or wish you weren't feeling, or general questions about your day or your life.

Be open to whatever comes up. Let the dialogue go where it will.

Take thirty seconds of silence for this conversation. Transcribe it if that will assist you. If you choose to write it down at this time, pause the recording until you're done. As you write, remember to remain in the flow of experience by writing without censoring or second-guessing, without stopping to correct, without stopping for any reason.

Now that you feel complete with that interaction, step forward. Take another step. Then another, moving closer and closer to your Wisest Self...until you step into your Wisest Self, until you and your Wisest Self become one, merging in a wondrous moment of divine union.

What does that feel like? What sensations or emotions run through you? What do you see? Sense? Hear? Intuit?

Breathe deeply into the merged entity you are and experience all there is to experience...feel all there is to feel...be all there is to be.

Take twenty seconds of clock time to experience this fully.

Now that you feel complete, step back and away from your Wisest Self. Note any feelings or sensations that action sparks for you. As you step away, thank your Wisest Self for assisting you today and allow your Wisest Self to respond.

Before you leave this place, your Wisest Self hands you a gift, an expression of appreciation for having been freed into your life more consciously. What is it?

Receive this gift and keep it with you.

Recall it, if you choose, every time you sit down to dialogue.

Now, turn back to the door — that special door — knowing that you can return to this place at any time to meet with your Wisest Self. All you need to do is remember how it felt to be here. All it takes is stillness. A quiet time. A quiet place, where you're free to envision, where it's safe to connect.

Once more, you touch the door, it swings open and you step through…and back.

As you return to your starting place, you bring back with you all that you sensed and all that you saw and all that you heard, felt and intuited. You're bringing it back to your conscious awareness, remembering whatever, in this moment, it serves you to remember.

When you're ready, but only then, open your eyes, staying with all you experienced.

Write about it — what you saw, felt or sensed. Write about the conversation you had with your Wisest Self. Write whatever you remember, whatever comes up, taking all the time you need.

Remember to keep your pen moving across the page. Remember to breathe. Remember to censor nothing, freeing the voice of your Wisest Self to live again through you on the page.

These additional recorded meditations from "The Voice of the Muse Companion" will also help you deepen your dialogue experiences:

- "Let Judgment Go"
- "Taming Your Critic"
- "Write the Feeling"

Grateful Appreciation

Too much time has passed since theses dialogues were first penned for me to be able to remember by name all those who touched my life and encouraged these writings back then. Not being able to be specific, however, does not dim my gratitude to the many who long ago passed out of my life but who, nonetheless, influence what you read on these pages.

Some names do thrust their way through the mists of time and memory: Jim and Angela Emery, more second family than landlords during the five months chronicled here; the Emerys' nine-year-old son, Jeremy, who taught me more than any adult master could; Barbara Sauvé, a bulwark of support during the weeks our Georgian Bay sojourns coincided; and Roxy, my cocker spaniel companion not only through my time in Penetanguishene but in the twenty-four months that followed.

If in late 1996 or early 1997 you were a patron or staffer at The Daily Perk cafe in Midland, Ontario, you were part of my sole social outlet during those months of retreat and I also owe you my gratitude.

Today I add a new round of thanks, to those who have supported this project, not always knowingly, over the nearly two decades since its unexpected birth: Joan Cerio, Sander Dov Freedman, Aalia Golden, Lee Graham, Kathleen Messmer (whose photographic genius produced this book's cover image), Karen Weaver and the many members of my spiritual family I encountered on the cross-continent and Sedona odysseys that followed almost immediately on the heels of these dialogues. Nor must I neglect the coffee-bar baristas in multiple US states who unknowingly kept me going on this book over the years or Kyri, Roxy's canine successor as I worked on this new edition. You'll see him in the author photo on the back cover of the paperback or above my bio in the ebook

My closest intimate through what would turn out to be my final Canadian winter was the land itself. To the shores and waters of Georgian Bay, whose energy sustained me during a period of darkness-into-light that mirrored Mother Nature's, thank you: You were the perfect backdrop for that transformative time.

Georgian Bay was not the only landscape that fed into *Dialogues with the Divine*. I worked on early drafts of this book in many places, among them the urban canyons of Toronto, the golden beaches of the Oregon coast, the red rocks of Sedona, the volcanic slopes of the Big Island of Hawaii and the Pacific shores of Maui. The granite outcroppings of New Mexico's Sandia Mountains watched over me as I completed the first *Dialogues* edition and the lively buzz of Portland's Pearl District supported me as I prepared the new edition you now hold in your hand.

Finally, to the Divine, who, like my Muse, is not some external "other" but the wisest and most powerful part of me: Thank you for words of encouragement and inspiration that remain as meaningful to me today as they were when they first dropped onto my page in the dark days of a Simcoe County winter.

An Exceptional Telling of an Exceptional Story!

Mark David Gerson never wanted to be a writer, never believed in a world beyond that of his five senses.

But when life began to chip away at his identity with a relentlessness that he couldn't ignore, he found himself launched on a spiritual journey that would redefine everything about him — multiple times.

It was a journey of surrender that ultimately birthed a timeless fantasy series…and a new life he could never have imagined.

A Journey of Singular Courage by a True Spiritual Master

When financial disaster forces Mark David Gerson from his Portland home with everything he owns packed into the back of his car, he launches an open-ended odyssey that will carry him from the Pacific to the Mississippi and back, never knowing from one day to the next whether he can muster the faith to keep going.

"A compelling read that will leave you feeling inspired and humbled."

www.ingramcontent.com/pod-product-compliance
Lightning Source LLC
Chambersburg PA
CBHW030108100526
44591CB00009B/323